CREATE IT WITH CREATESPACE

A GUIDE TO SELF PUBLISHING YOUR BOOK WITH AMAZON'S FREE PUBLISHING SERVICE

JOEL ADAMS

CREATE IT WITH CREATESPACE
A guide to self publishing your book with Amazon's free publishing service.

ISBN-13: 978-1505470000

ISBN-10: 1505470005

TABLE OF CONTENTS

PART I
GETTING STARTED

INTRODUCTION

Thanks for picking up *Create it with CreateSpace.*

Throughout this book you'll learn the basics of self-publishing a book through Amazon's free publishing platform: CreateSpace.

Aspiring authors are everywhere, but the idea of getting published is sometimes such a daunting task that many people don't even write their book, let alone publish it.

CreateSpace is a platform to publish your paperback absolutely free!

While there are some *optional* costs you can choose to do, you could potentially publish a book and literally spend no money. Zero. Zilch. Nada.

The only optional expenses are purchasing a paperback copy of your proof (generally only a few bucks with shipping) and doing the expanded distribution ($25).

With costs like that, there's really no risk!

This book is, naturally, published and created with CreateSpace.

So just by reading this book, you are getting a glimpse at the quality of books you can create and sell, all at zero or minimal cost.

This book tackles the basics of publishing with CreateSpace. You'll learn how to get a free ISBN with CreateSpace, format your book's interior properly in Microsoft Word as well as how to create your book cover - either a basic one using CreateSpace's built in system, or a little more advanced version with Photoshop (or a similar program).

Don't worry, if you're truly having trouble with your cover, you can always hire a designer to help you out!

THE TOOLS

When formatting your book, there a few things you're going to need to get the ball rolling.

The required things are:

- A Computer (OK this was a bit obvious)
- Microsoft Word (2007 version preferably)

That's all you really *need* to publish with CreateSpace and work through this book.

While Microsoft Word 2007 is the *preferred* version (and the version I'll be using when explaining formatting) any version over version 2003 should suffice, it will just require a little bit more Google searching on your part.

This book also assumes a basic level of computer knowledge. When I ask you to sign up for CreateSpace I expect that you can enter your own information and verify your account from your email.

The optional tools in this book are:

- Adobe Photoshop

As you can see, it's not an extensive list! I'll be using Photoshop CS5 for my tutorials on the cover. However, if you don't have it, or can't get it, a similar program called "GIMP" is available for free. Give it a quick Google search and you'll find it.

One warning about Photoshop and especially GIMP is that these programs require some know how to really manipulate the graphics.

You can always find tutorials online, but for the purposes of this book, I'm going to assume a basic level of skill when using Photoshop (or GIMP).

If you can't manage it, you can try hiring someone online to design you a cover (you'd be surprised how cheap you can get one made if you dig) or use the cover designer built into the CreateSpace website.

Without further ado, let's get cracking on how to *Create it with CreateSpace!*

SIGNING UP ON CREATESPACE.COM

The first thing you're going to need to do is, of course, sign up for a CreateSpace.com account!

To do this, open your browser and go to http://www.createspace.com

Simply click the "Sign Up" link to get started.

Continue to follow the steps to complete your sign up. You'll also be asked to verify your email address.

Check your inbox for a confirmation email and simply click the supplied link to verify your account. If you don't get it, you can simply click the "Resend email" button.

Please Verify Your Email Address

Thanks, your CreateSpace member sign-up is almost complete. Just one more step to get you started.

An email with a confirmation code was sent to ▆▆▆▆▆▆▆▆ [Resend email]

To verify your email address, be sure to:

| Click on the link in the verification email | **OR** | Enter and verify the confirmation code |
| | | [ ] [Submit] |

About Us   Contact Us   Affiliates   Twitter   Facebook   Press Room

Terms of Use   Member Agreement   Privacy   Sitemap   Careers   Copyright © 2000 - 2013, CreateSpace, a DB

Great, now you should be logged in and ready to create a title with CreateSpace.

CREATE YOUR BOOK

When logged in you should be at the "Member Dashboard" page. Click the navy blue "Add New Title" button to get started.

Now, you're going to fill out a few details about your project, including the name of your book and the type of project (Paperback) you're doing.

Finally, you'll choose a setup process. Definitely stick with the Guided setup as it's simpler and doesn't really offer any real advantage over the Expert setup process.

Click the "Get Started" button to proceed to the next step.

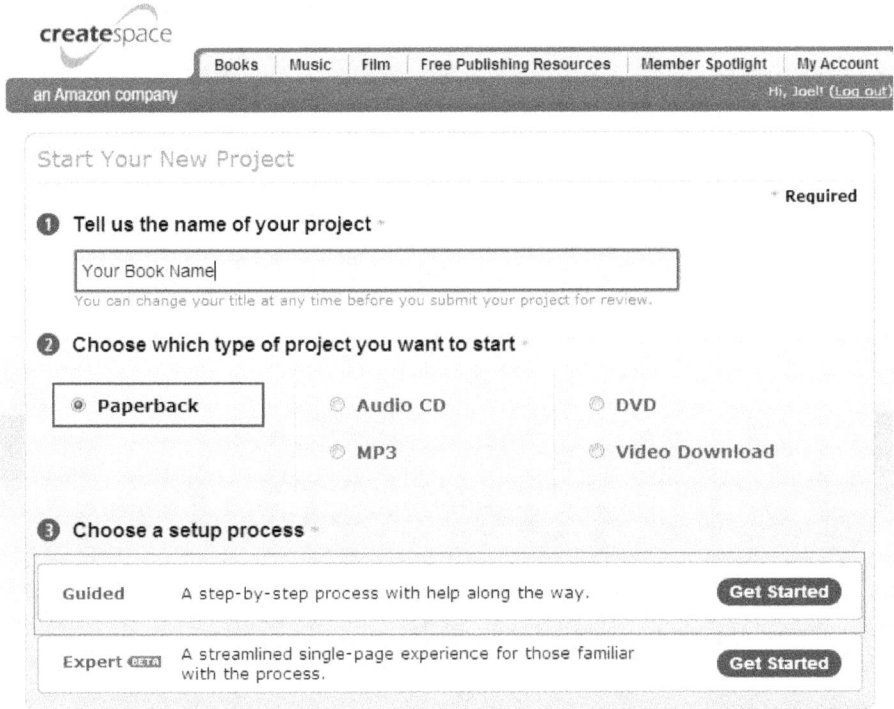

Now you'll have to fill in some more details about your book including the Subtitle (if applicable), Author, other contributors (again, if applicable), whether it's part of a series or not (you can change this at a later date if needed). You can also optionally put in an Edition number (again, you can edit this later if needed).

Finally, you must select the language and then you can select a Publication date. It's probably best to leave the Publication date blank since you don't really know when your book will be published. My understanding is this is really for books that were published elsewhere at a previous date or are a second edition or the like.

After you've filled out all of that info, click the "Save & Continue" button.

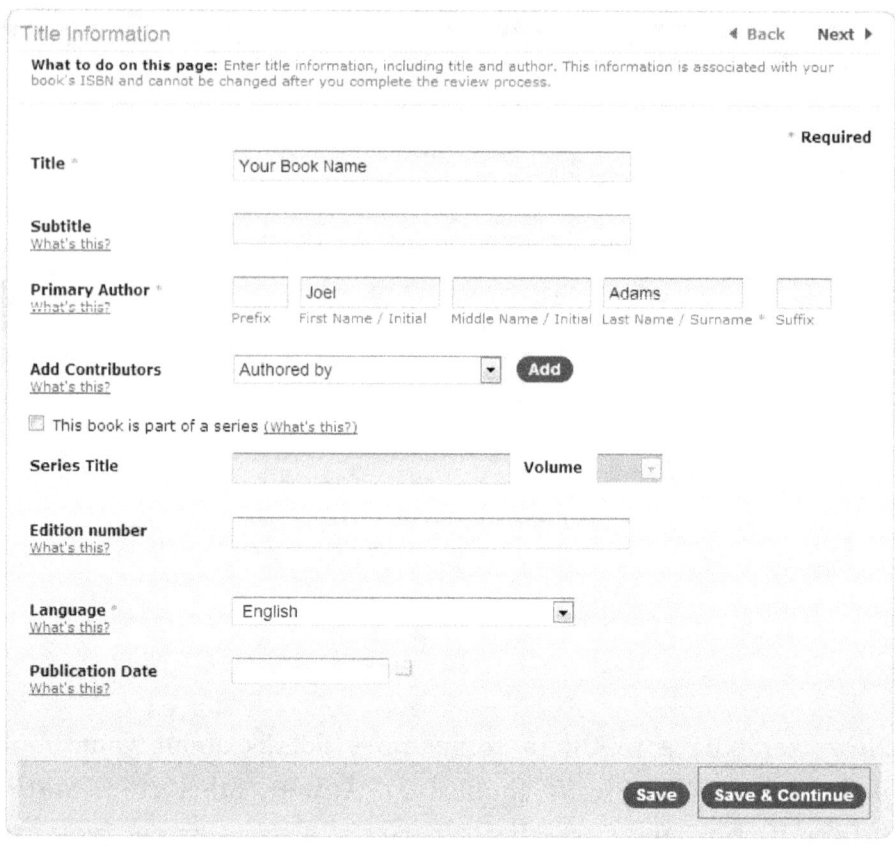

ISBN NUMBER

Now you'll be presented with the ISBN page.

CreateSpace will assign a free ISBN to your book, and for the purposes of this book this is the only option I'll be covering since providing your own can become complex. This is intended to be a beginning guide and not advanced so only the free option will be covered.

So, select the "Free CreateSpace-Assigned ISBN" bullet and then click the "Assign Free ISBN" button to continue to the next step.

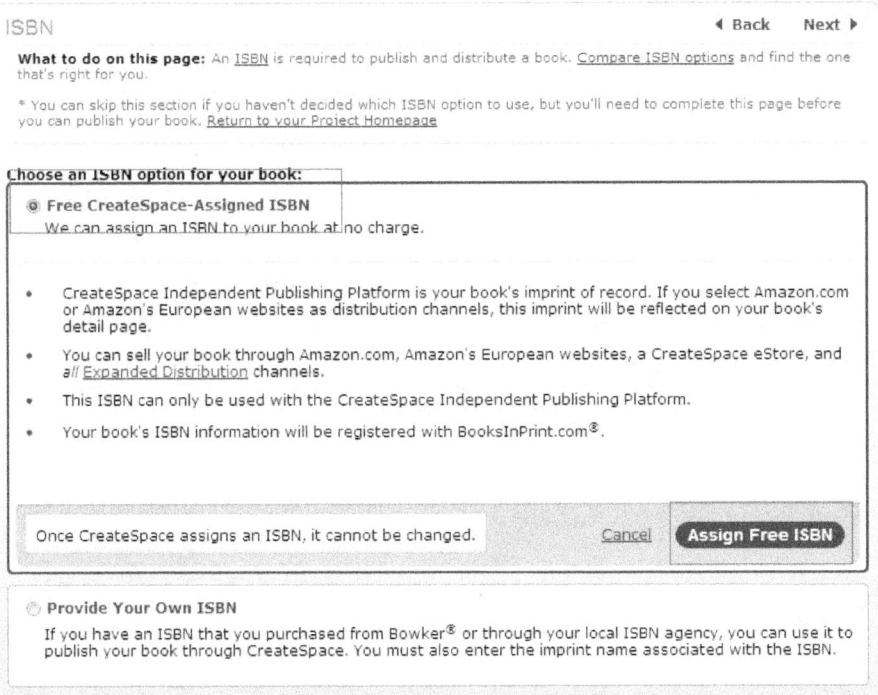

Next you'll get a screen that shows you your newly assigned ISBN numbers:

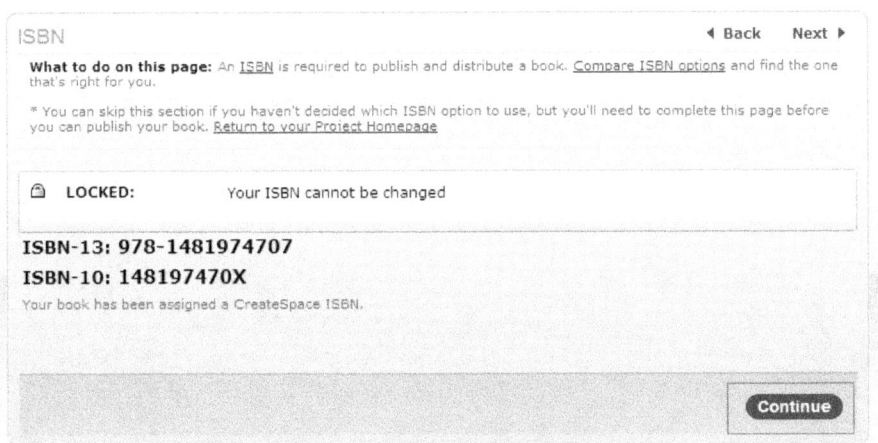

The ISBN-13 is the more universally recognized number, and is the only one you really need to worry about, although some people like to use the ISBN-10 as well.

To be safe, save the numbers to a file on your computer for future use. You're going to want these on the copyright page of your book.

For now, you're done with CreateSpace.com and you won't be coming back until your book interior is formatted. Move onto the next chapter and get started!

PART II
THE INTERIOR

BASIC INTERIOR FORMATTING

Formatting your book interior can be easy in some ways, yet extremely frustrating in others.

The best thing you can do is use a properly formatted template from the get go; instead of trying to modify your existing one.

This is bad news if you already have your manuscript done, but it's certainly not the end of the world. If your book is already done, you'll have to make some fixes along the way, although it's definitely doable.

MARGINS, GUTTERS, HEADERS AND FOOTERS

The most important thing to do to your document is format your margins, gutter, header and footer properly.

Luckily this is quite easy. No matter what size book you are printing, these values will *always* be the same.

Top Margin	0.75"
Bottom Margin	0.75"
Inside Margin	0.75"
Outside Margin	0.5"
Gutter	0.13"
Header/Footer	0.35"

To format these things click the "Page Layout" tab, then click "Margins" then click "Custom Margins". See the image below for easier reference.

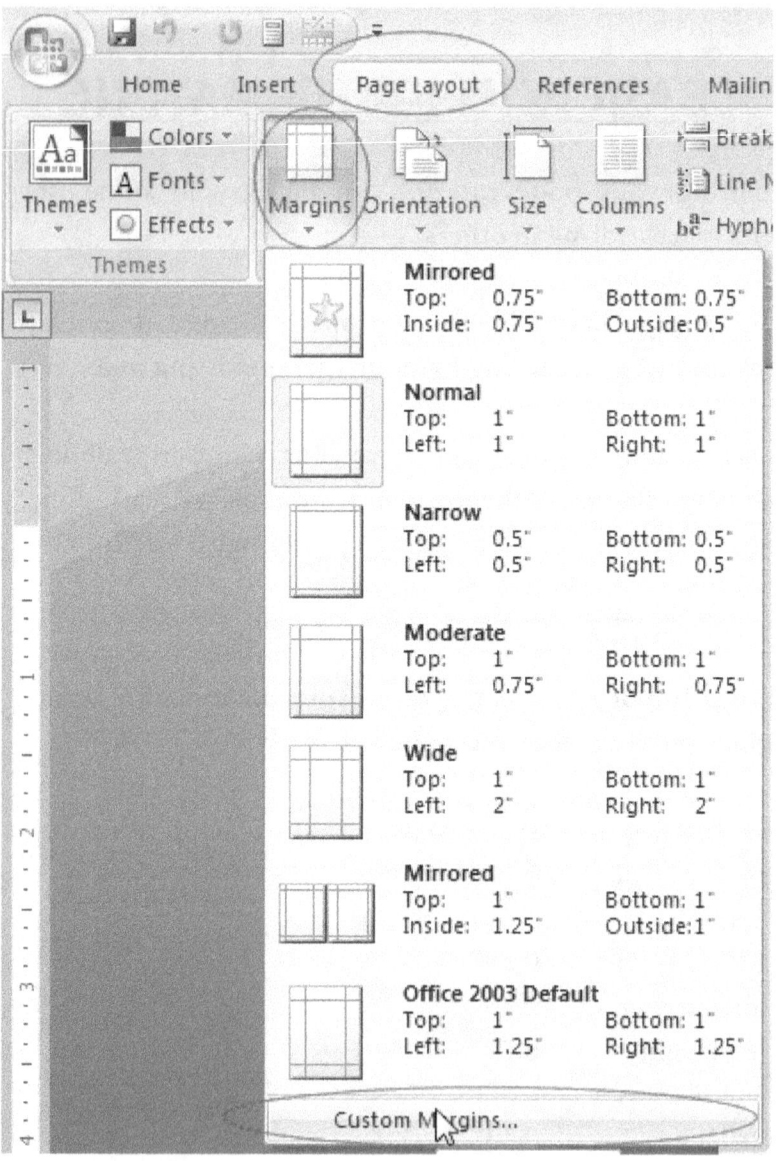

From here you will be presented with the Page Setup window. Enter the values I already gave you and also make sure you select "Mirror Margins" and "Whole Document". Your values should look like the picture below when you're done:

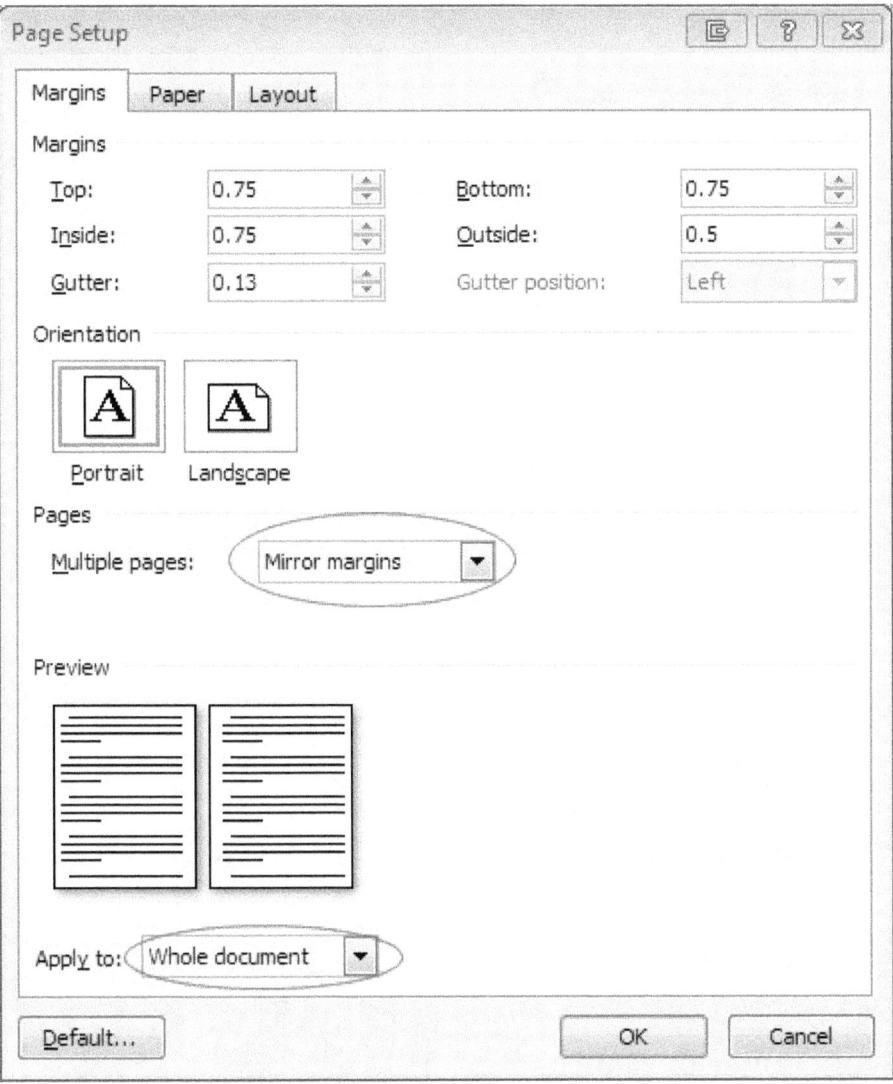

This just leaves the Headers and Footers. Leaving your Page Setup window open, click the "Layout" tab. Enter your Header and Footer information here and note the circled items. I'll go over those shortly as well:

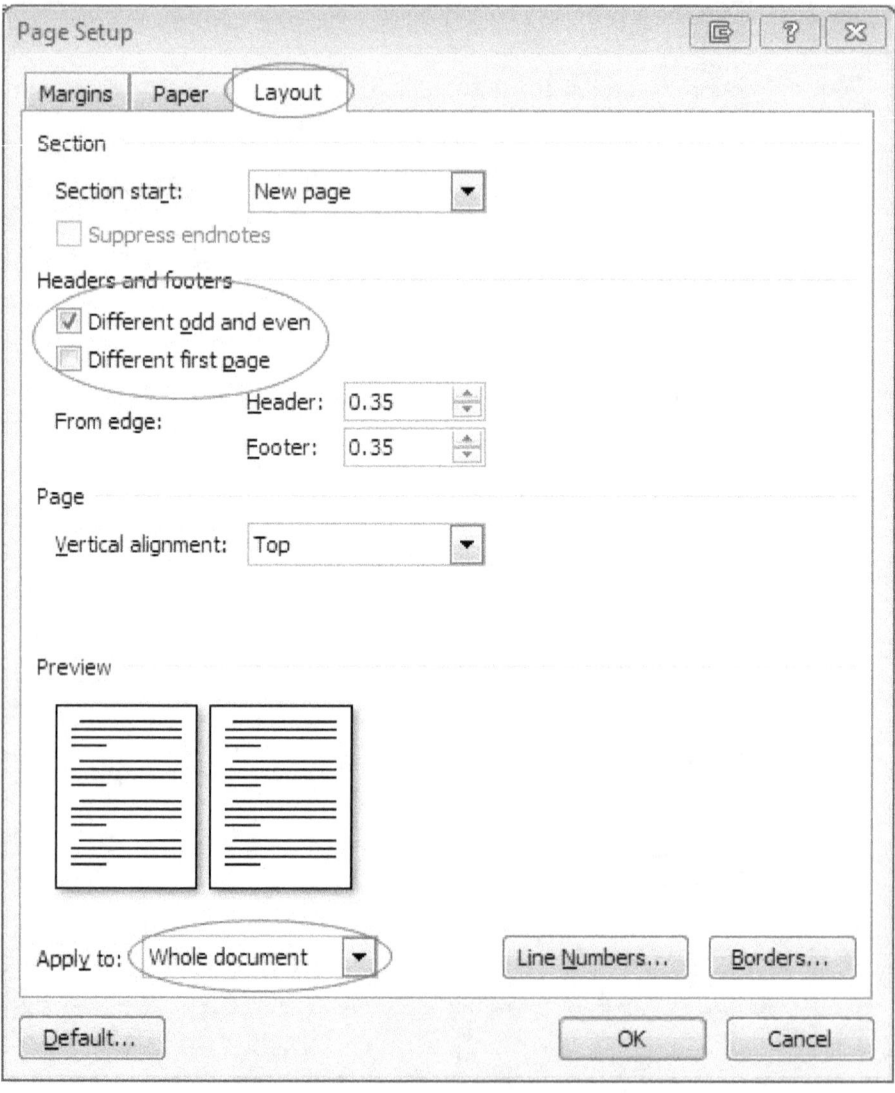

As with your Margins and Gutters, make sure "Whole Document" is selected.

You'll notice a couple different options as well:

- Different odd and even
- Different first page

These are completely optional settings. The reason you'd want your header and footer to be different on *odd and even* pages is so you can number your pages on the outside edge of each page and also so you can have differing information on each header/footer if you like.

Take this book for example. All of the odd page headers have my name (author name) as well as the page number on the right hand side. This is because odd numbered pages are always on the right hand side of your book when being read. Then, the even pages in this book have the page number and the book title in the left corner. This is for the same reason; even numbered pages are always on the left side of a book when opened. This way the header is always on the *outside* of each page.

It's not necessary to have the author name and book title in the header, and can actually make things more difficult. I recommend staying away from it if you're a beginner. However having the page number on the outside edges is something you may want to do, and if so, make sure you check the "Different odd and even" box in the Layout tab (pictured previously).

If you'd rather just have the page numbers centered at the top or bottom of your page, don't check this box.

The option "Different first page" is a bit more complicated. I did use it in this book. If you flip back to the start of this chapter, you'll notice that that first page with the chapter title has the page number in the *footer* instead of the header and it's centered. There's also nothing in the header. Again, this is quite common, although not completely necessary to have a professional quality book. Trust me, no one will really notice if you don't have a different first page.

A different first page also requires using *section breaks* in Word. This is not something I cover in this book as sections can be quite difficult. If you're familiar with sections and section breaks in Word, or you want to put in some extra time in with Google searching to learn it, then you could check this box and have at it!

One final note on the headers, footers, margins and gutter: I highly recommend sticking to the default numbers for these things, but if for some reason you want to have different numbers, you can do so but *only* make these values *higher*, never lower.

So if you wanted more white space on edges of your page you might change the Inside Margin to 1" and the Outside Margin to 0.75".

This is typically just a waste of space, and the only reason you'd want to do this is to increase your page count. Some people view longer books as being more worth their money, but remember the more pages you have in your book, the more you have to charge to make decent royalties.

For the purposes of this book, we're assuming default values for these things.

Now that everything is formatted, it is time to put your page numbers in.

PAGE NUMBERS

When inserting page numbers, you have to consider if you're going to do page numbers in the same position on every page (centered works best) or different odd and even so that the page numbers can be on the outer edge of each printed page.

Putting page numbers in your header or footer is quite easy.

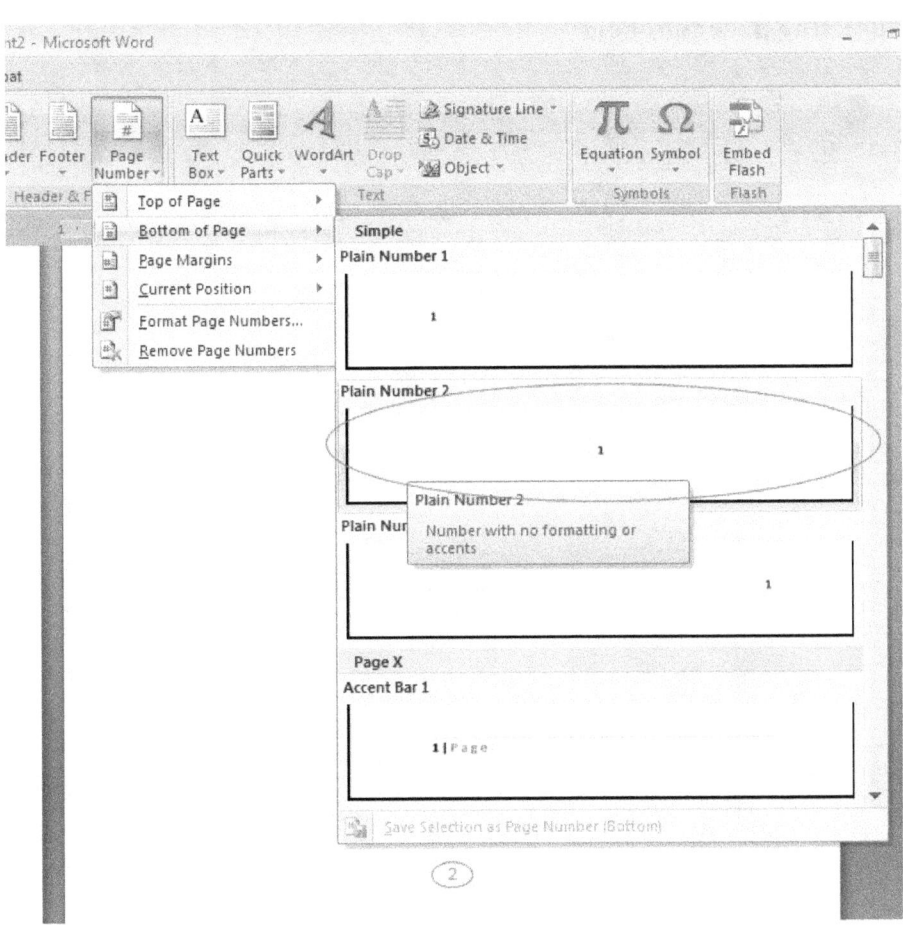

The previous picture illustrates how to insert a page number into the footer of your book (centered).

First click the "Insert" tab in Word 2007, then "Page Number" then select the style of number and position you want. The last example is best used when the odd and even pages are the same (so the "Different odd and even" box is *not* checked).

The following example demonstrates how to do page numbers on the outer edge of each page (having the "Different odd and even" box *checked* in this example) and use the same method as before for inserting page numbers.

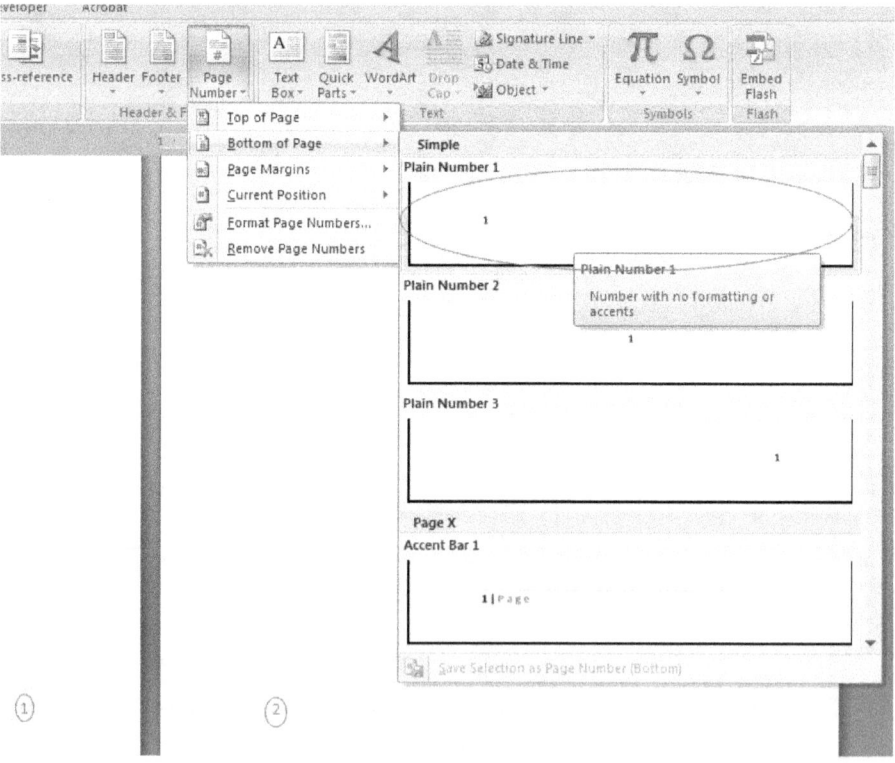

You'll have to do this twice: once for the odd pages and once for the even pages. As you can see the odd page (page 1) has the number on the right hand side and the even numbered page (page 2) has it on the left hand side of the page. This means, when printed the number will always appear on the outside edge of the each page. This is my preferred method, although it's strictly preference. As I mentioned before, this is how the page numbers are done in this book (with the exception of the first page of each chapter).

That's it! As I said, inserting the page numbers is very easy. You can get into more complex options such as roman numerals on the first few pages followed by regular numbers after, but this involves using section breaks, which as I mentioned before are a more advanced formatting technique and not covered in this book. If you're willing to put in the effort, you can certainly do this in Microsoft Word.

STYLES

Styles are an extremely important part of your formatting. It both keeps your formatting consistent and helps you make a dynamic table of contents.

A dynamic table of contents is one of the best things you can have. It will allow you to have Word automatically update the page numbers without you having to fix them every time you make a change.

You'll want to utilize *at least* two styles: "Heading 1" and "Normal" but you can use as many as you want.

You should utilize the "Heading 1" style for your chapter headings. This is again for the purpose of the dynamic table of contents. You can easily generate a table of contents that will add entries for every "Heading 1" in your book.

If it sounds confusing now, it will become clear later.

However, for now formatting your "Normal" style is the first thing you want to do. This will be the font style and size that you use for the main parts of your book. The sentence you're reading right now is my "Normal" style.

I've chosen the font "Minion Pro Smbd" and a font size of 12. So the first thing I'd do is select that font in my Word Document. Once you've selected your font, I want you type a sentence, any sentence will do.

Now, your "Normal" Style is still not the way you want it, but that is easily fixed. Simply highlight the text you just wrote (the text that is the font and size you want). Now right click your "Normal" style up in your Style toolbar and then click "Update Normal to Match Selection. Now your "Normal" style is the way you want it.

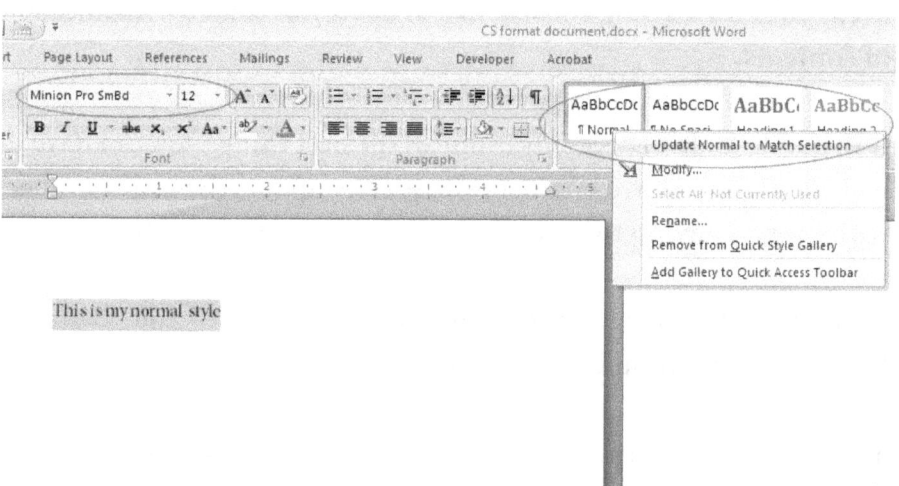

I also recommend using the "Justify" style so your text will be justified to fit the page the best way possible.

The best part is that if you ever decide to change your font and/or size, you only need to change your "Normal" style and everything in your entire book formatted as "Normal" will automatically be updated to reflect the new font and/or size.

This way of changing your style goes for all styles in Microsoft Word.

For your chapter headings, you'd also type something in the font size and style you want and then update the Heading 1 style to match that selection in the same way you did for the Normal style.

You can also make sub-chapter headings (use Heading 2), and any other styles that are different than your Normal such as for quotes that are formatted differently than your Normal text.

Once you master making use of Styles, your formatting will not only be 100% consistent, it will be much, much easier to handle all the various fonts styles and sizes in your book.

TABLE OF CONTENTS

Congrats! This is the last section about the interior formatting, and if you've followed everything so far, this will be a piece of cake!

The reason it's so easy is that if you've formatted all of your headings as "Heading 1" (and "Heading 2" if applicable) then your Table of Contents (TOC) can be generated with just a few clicks!

Take a look at the TOC in this book: it was generated with a few clicks. I made a couple additions (the PART I, PART II, etc.) but in essence it's just that easy.

All of my chapter headings are in "Heading 1" and this chapter is called "Basic Interior Formatting". The subheadings (like the "Table of Contents" sub-heading you just saw) are all formatted as "Heading 2".

I'm sure you're dying to add your TOC, so I'll show you how to insert it now!

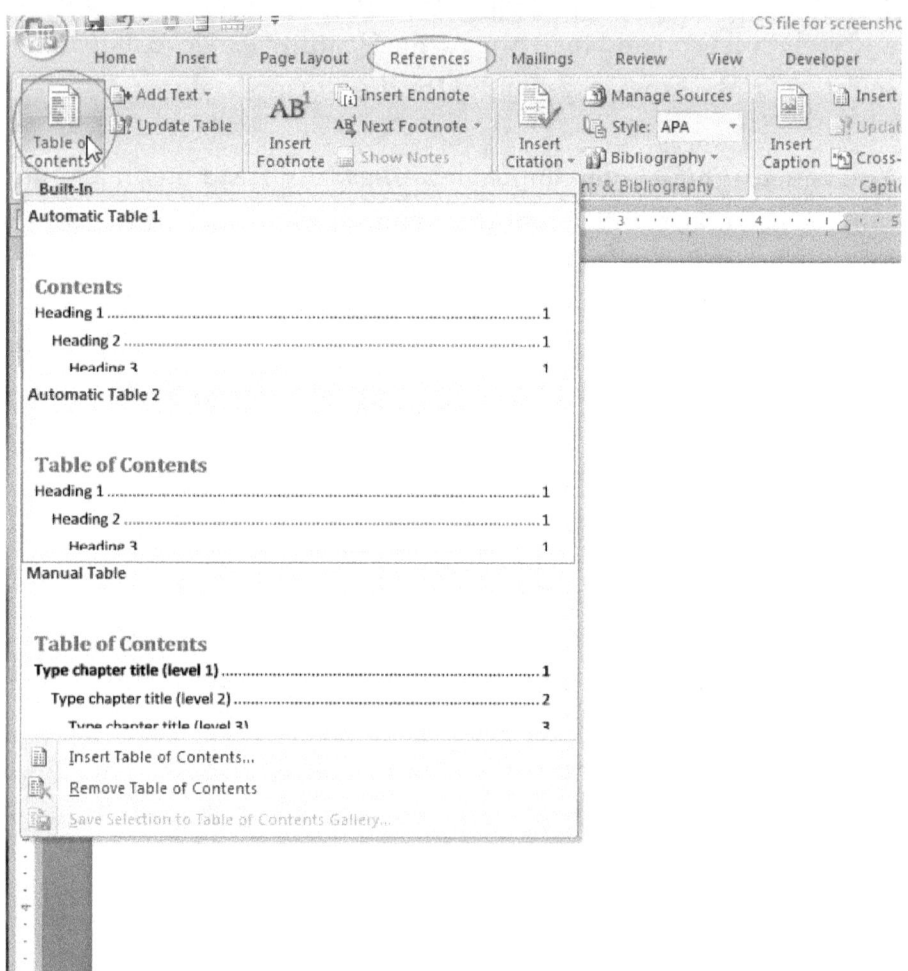

It's easy! All you have to do is select the "References" tab, then click the "Table of Contents" button.

You'll be presented with two different Automatic Tables; stick to these. The only difference between the two is that one says "Contents" and one says "Table of Contents". Really this doesn't matter because you can just change it to whatever you want anyway. So go ahead and select either one and see your table of contents automatically generate.

If you did it right it should look something like this:

Contents
INTRODUCTION 3
CHAPTER 1 – This is formatted as Heading 1 5
    Sub-heading in chapter 1 formatted as heading 2 6
Chapter 2 – This chapter has no sub-headings 8
Chapter 3 – This chapter has two sub-headings 9
    This is one 10
    And this is the other 11

Congratulations, you now have a *dynamic* TOC. Dynamic TOC's will make your life very easy. You'll find out why later; for now, you probably want to change the way your Table of Contents looks!

Chances are you don't want the default fonts and the blue heading for your TOC. You can change the formatting just like any other text, so go nuts. You can also change the title to anything. See the example TOC again but with the formatting changed to the way I want it. I'm going to center my title and call it "Book Contents", and change its font to Arial. I am also going to bold the Chapter entries, and change the font to Georgia. Lastly, I'll actually change the Introduction entry text. Even though in my book the heading is formatted simply as "Introduction" I can change the entry text to be whatever I want it to be.

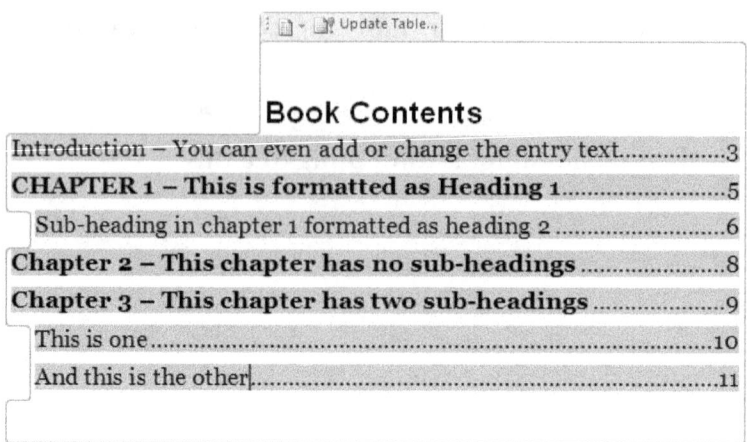

This is all quite easy, you can even add text in between entries if you want, like I did in the TOC in the following example:

Book Contents

Now I'll move on to show you why the dynamic table of contents is so great.

Most likely you're going to put in your TOC before you final edits. Or at least you'll have some edits *after* your "final" edit :)

So what do you do when you insert a new chapter or even just one lousy paragraph that throws off the page numbers of every chapter from that point forward in your TOC?

Luckily, since your TOC is dynamic, you don't have to worry too much. I'll be using my TOC example again, but note that chapter 2 will be pushed to page 10.

Now since it's only the page numbers that need updating, I'll show you how to update page numbers only first.

- Right click anywhere in your table of contents
- Select "Update Field"
- Select "Update page numbers only"
- Hit OK

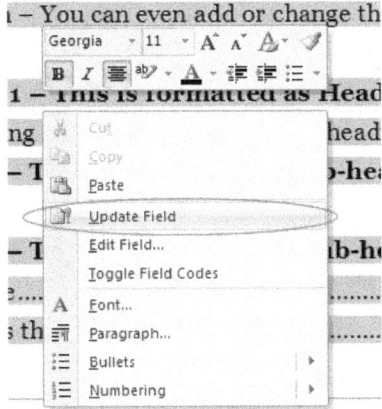

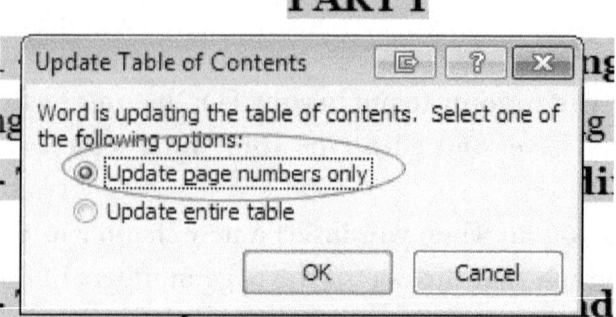

You'll probably use this all the time, and look, my table has automatically the page numbers for Chapter 2 and beyond:

Book Contents

That's the simple part!

Now, let's say that you not only add some new text but you also add a new chapter or sub-heading.

This is just as easy to update your TOC. Follow the same steps as before, but instead of clicking "Update page numbers only" click "Update entire table" and hit OK.

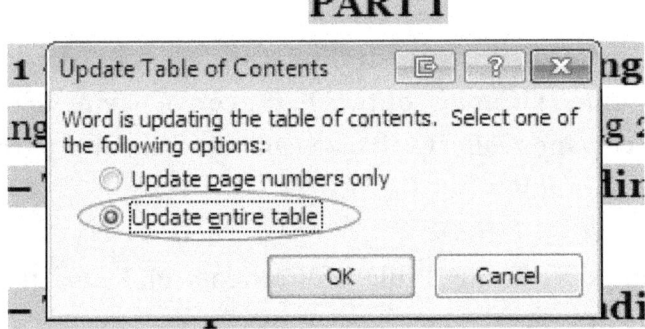

Now there is one annoying thing that happens when you do this. You'll generally lose all or some of the formatting you did to your table.

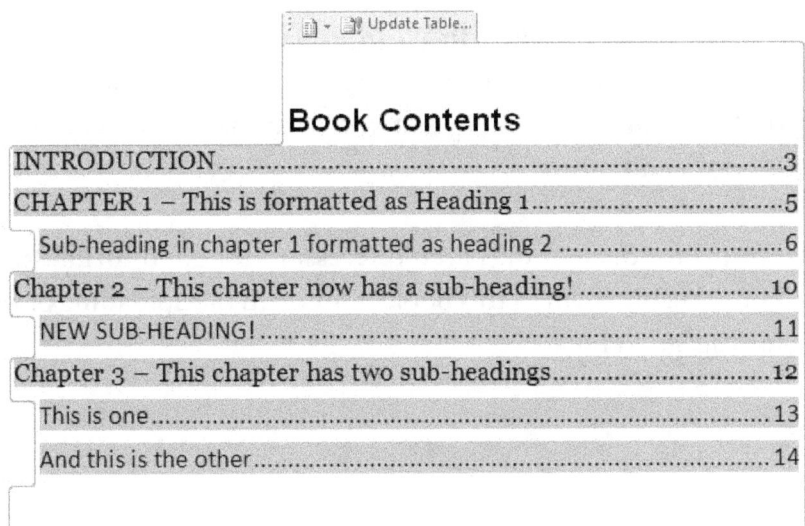

As you can see, it automatically inserted the "NEW SUBHEADING!" entry, but most of my formatting is gone.

Also gone are the "PART I" and "PART II" that I manually added.

This is an unfortunate fact of dealing with TOC's in Word. The pro's of the dynamic TOC much outweigh the con of having to reformat if you update it; and really it will take you only moments to reformat it the way you want it.

That about covers the Table of Contents and also the interior formatting in general!

Depending on how comfortable you are with Word, the interior formatting can be the most daunting task of all. I know it was for me! However, once you learn some of the basics of formatting you'll find it can become quite simple.

If you're very comfortable with Word, you can also experiment with some of the things I mentioned earlier like Headers or Footers with a different first page, alternating text next to the page numbers (such as in this book) and more.

However, since those things aren't necessary for good formatting, I won't be covering them in this book. Now on to the uploading of your interior file, good luck!

UPLOADING YOUR BOOK INTERIOR

Now that you have your book interior formatted the way you want it, it's time to upload it to CreateSpace.

This can be one of the most frustrating things there is, and I'll tell you why. Although CreateSpace supports uploading plain old Microsoft Word documents, it almost always changes something slightly.

This slight change can mess up your page numbers, and then all of a sudden your TOC is wrong! I've also seen it move footnotes to the *NEXT* page. So the superscript reference (like this[1]) is on the right page but the footnote is actually in the footer of the *NEXT* page.

Luckily there is a trick to getting it to come out *exactly* as you want, and after I learned this my life became much easier.

All you have to do is convert your Word Document to a PDF and use the PDF to upload to CreateSpace.

For whatever reason, a PDF uploaded on CreateSpace comes out the way it should and a Word Document does not.

So, the first thing you must do is create a PDF from your Word document.

SAVING YOUR FILE AS A PDF

First, download the free add-on allowing you to save a Word Document as a PDF.

This can be found for free at: http://www.microsoft.com/en-us/download/details.aspx?id=7 or if you'd rather not type all of that out, just Google "save as pdf word 2007" and you'll find it.

Close your Word 2007 program, then download and install the add-on. Now, re-open your file.

Now, you need to save it as a PDF. This is easy, simply click the Office button, hover over "Save As" and click "PDF or XPS"

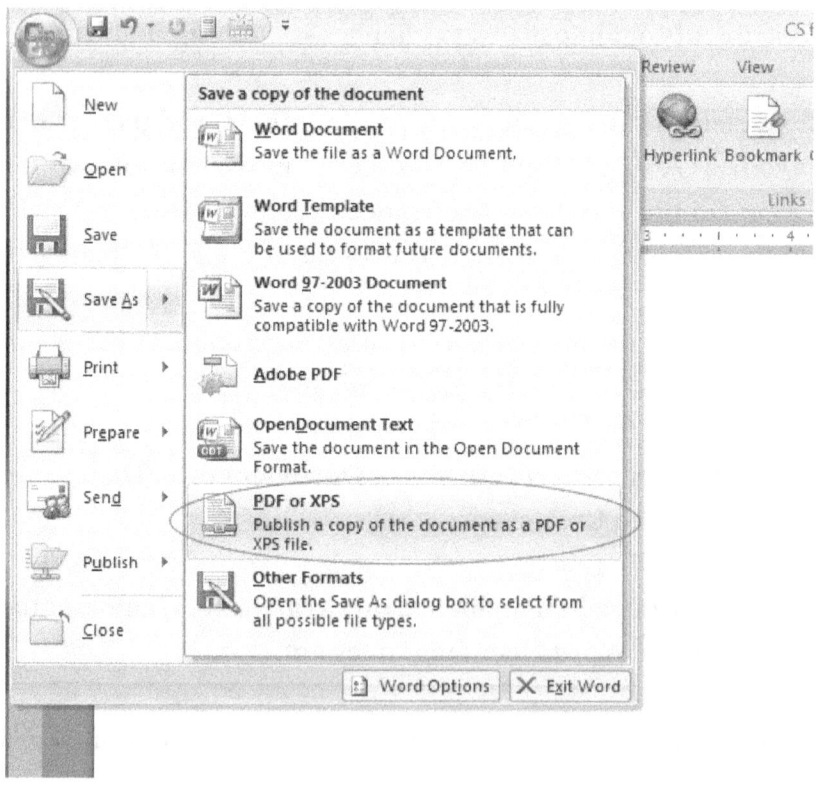

Now, in the save dialog box, you need to first click "Options" then select the "ISO 19005-1 compliant (PDF/A)" checkbox.

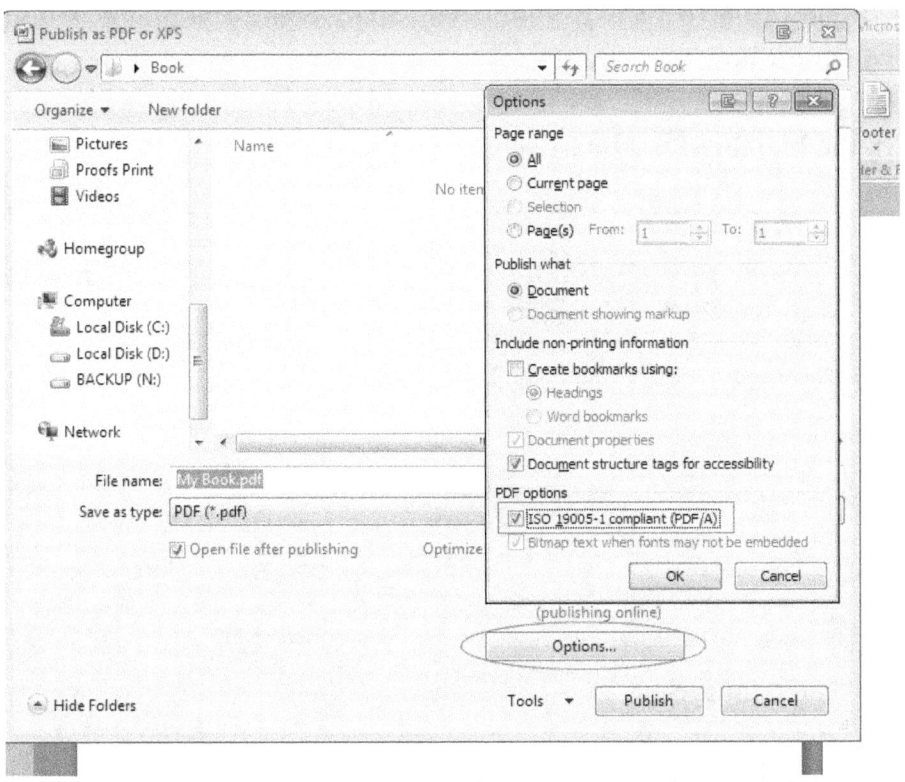

Then simply choose where to save your file and hit "Publish" to save the PDF.

That's it; you should have a PDF of your book now. Do a quick check on a few of the TOC entries to make sure the page numbers are still lining up (tip: the TOC is clickable in the PDF) and then you're ready to upload!

UPLOAD YOUR PDF

OK, now time to log in to your CreateSpace.com account. I'll assume you know how to do that!

In the Member Dashboard, click your book:

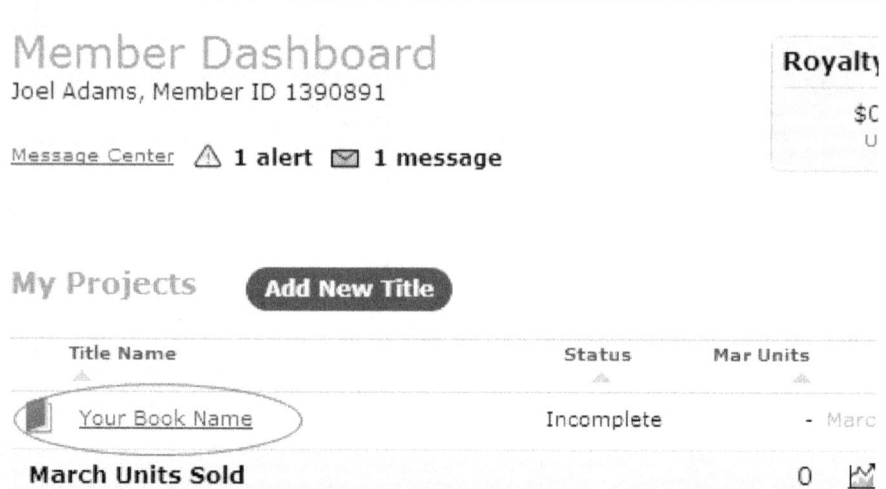

This should bring you to "Your Project" Homepage. From there, click the "Interior" link (it should have a red minus sign next to it at this point).

Now, make sure the appropriate book size and interior page type are selected. You should have already decided on the size, now decide if you want white or cream paper (you must use white if it has any color in the interior though).

Then you'll need to go to the Interior section and next to "Interiror File" select "Browse" to locate your PDF (*not* your Word document!).

Interior How do I use this page?

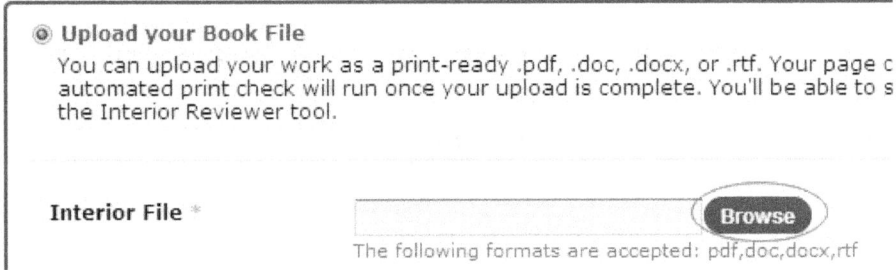

Browse to your PDF and upload it. It will ask you if the interior ends before the end of the page or after the end of the page. For the purposes of this book, always select "Ends before the edge of the page". The only time you'd use the other option (which is called "full bleed") would be if you were doing a book with pictures going right to the very edge of the page. Not only is this rare but costs *a lot* more.

So again, select that option and then hit "Save".

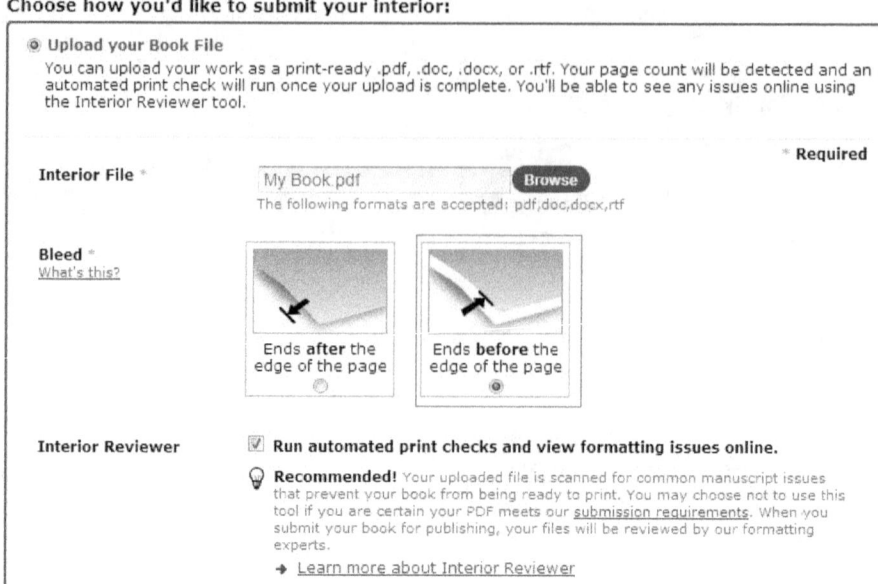

After that, you will be presented with several progress bars while it does its automated checks. This usually takes a few minutes depending on the size of your book.

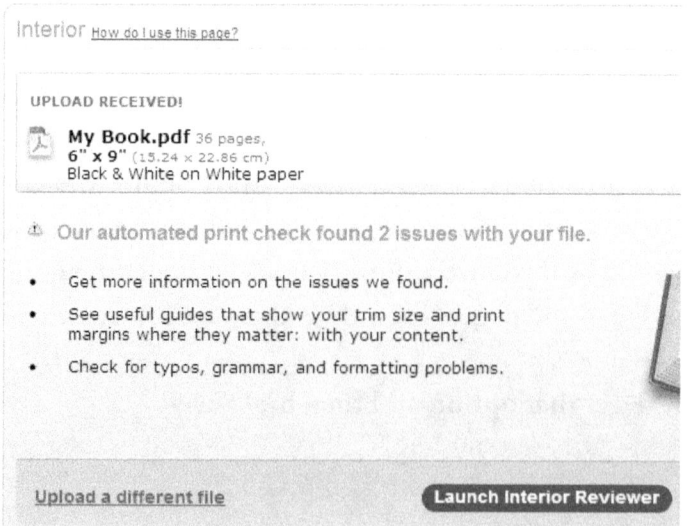

You very likely *will* have issues found with your book, so launch the Interior Reviewer.

The Interior Reviewer will show you your issues in the top right corner:

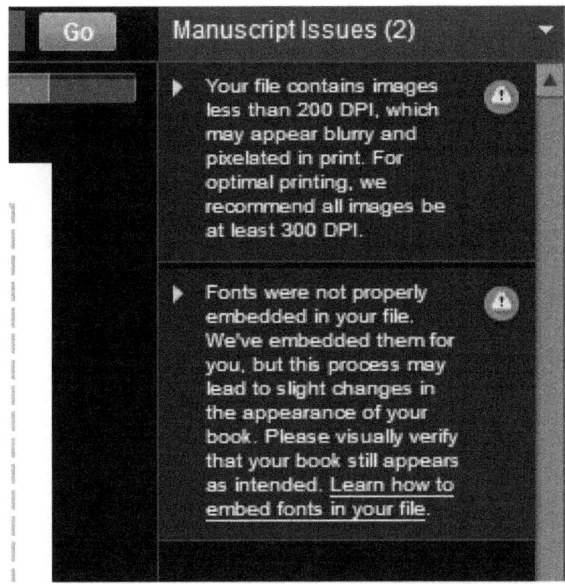

If you click on each issue, it will show you what page(s) the issue occurs on. The two in this example are the most common and the *only* issues you should encounter if you created your file right.

The first issue is that it found images with lower resolution than 200DPI. Although not ideal, this is more a matter of preference than anything. If you have pictures in your book and encounter this issue, I suggest looking at your interior PDF at 100% zoom in your PDF viewer and maybe printing a page or two on your home printer. If the images are acceptable to you in those two cases, they will be acceptable to you on your final book.

The other issue is that it *might* say the Fonts were not properly embedded. This rarely causes issue. Essentially all you have to do is take a quick look through your interior on the Interior Reviewer and see if anything looks off (in terms of the font). If it's to your satisfaction (and it should be) then you're all set.

Once you feel comfortable that the interior is OK, click "Save and Continue" at the bottom. You'll be taken back to the previous page only now there will be a button called "Ignore Issues and Continue". Click it.

That's it; your interior is now uploaded to CreateSpace! With that out of the way, you're now going to have to take care of the cover.

PART III
THE COVER

CREATESPACE'S FREE COVER CREATOR

Creating your cover can be the most daunting task of your book. The cover is the first thing people see when looking at your book, and even though we've all been told to "not judge a book by its cover" that is something we all do!

CreateSpace.com does supply a free basic "Cover Creator" that you can choose to do online. It is limited and somewhat simplistic, but if you put enough effort into it, you can still end up with a professional cover for sure.

For my purposes, I have only used the Cover Creator once. I prefer to design my own, so my Cover Creator experience is little, however, I will still walk you through the steps of doing a basic cover. If you want to spend the time on it to really make it look great, you should be able to do so after reading this chapter.

If you're not already logged in to CreateSpace, log in now. Click your book title and then click "Cover" (again, this should have a red minus sign next to it).

From there you are going to click the "Build Your Cover Online" bullet and then click "Launch Cover Creator".

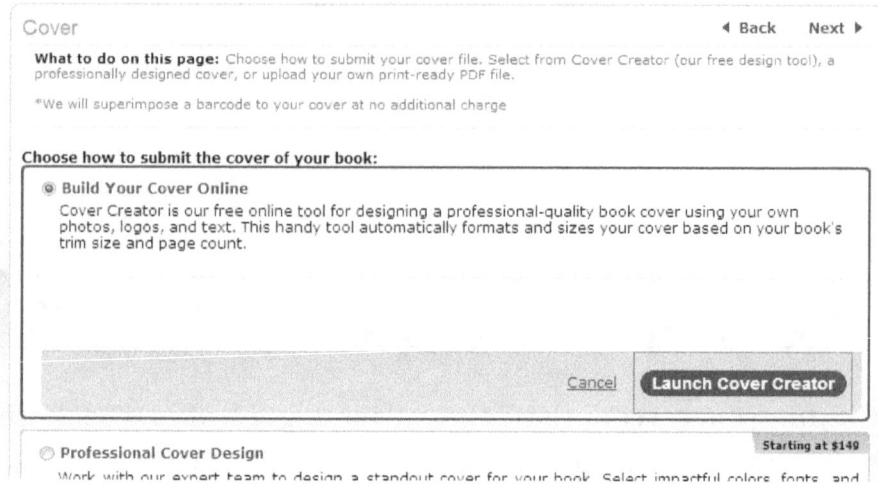

At this point, CreateSpace will present you with several pages of templates. Browse the templates and find the one you'd like to use as a starting point. You can change any pictures once you start editing it and also the color of the book, so try and keep that in mind when selecting your design.

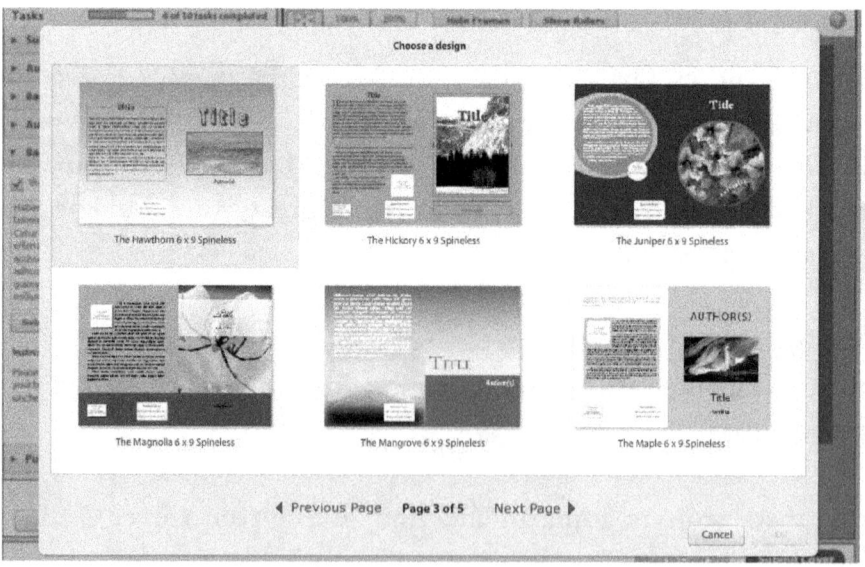

I've chosen "The Hawthorn" as my base template.

Now that I have my theme, Cover Creator brings me to the editor. The Name of the book and author name are already populated and the back has filler text in it.

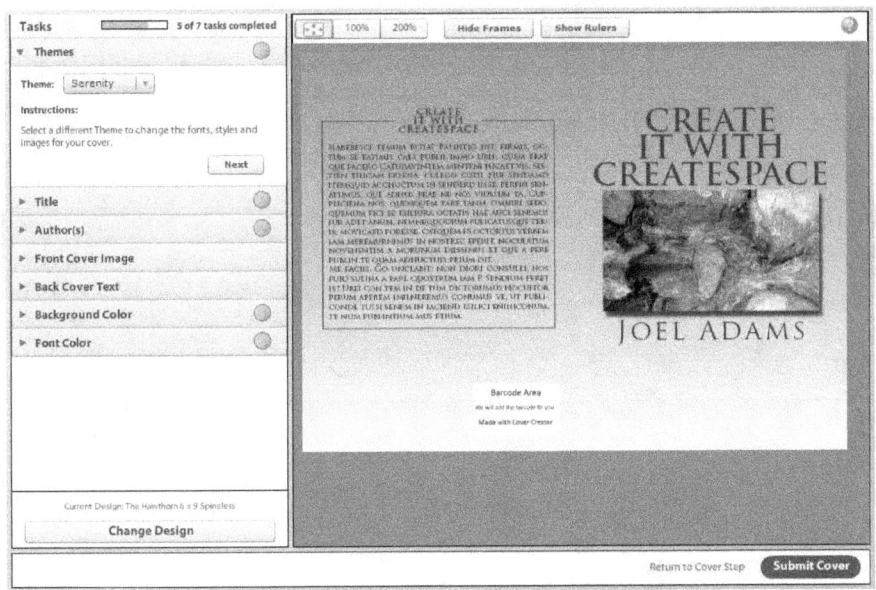

I don't want to use the supplied photo, so I'm going to upload my own.

To do this, I first navigate to "Front Cover Image" on the left hand side then click "Upload". Please read the Instructions regarding file size and quality before you upload your image.

Alternatively, you can click "Use one of our images" and browse through a wide variety of stock photos that CreateSpace supplies for free.

See the next page for pictures of both options.

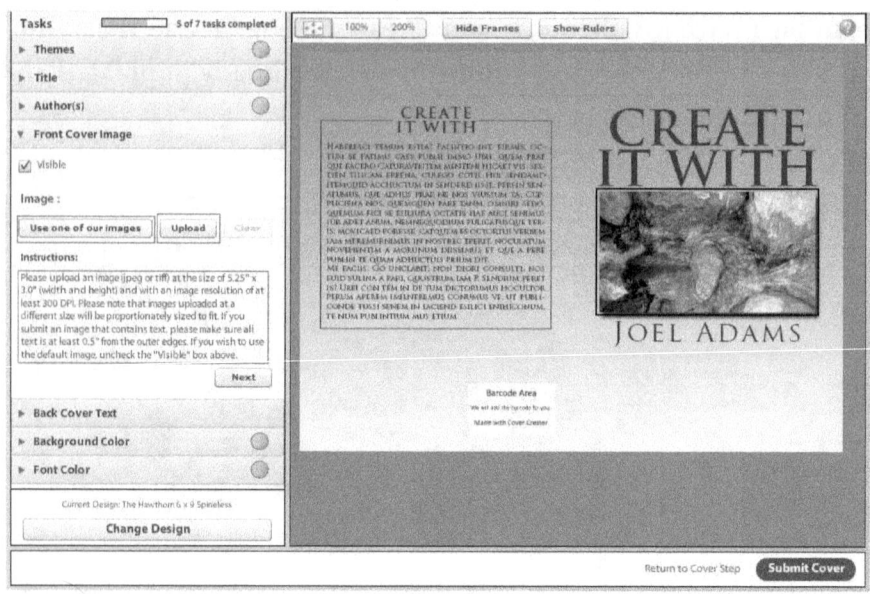

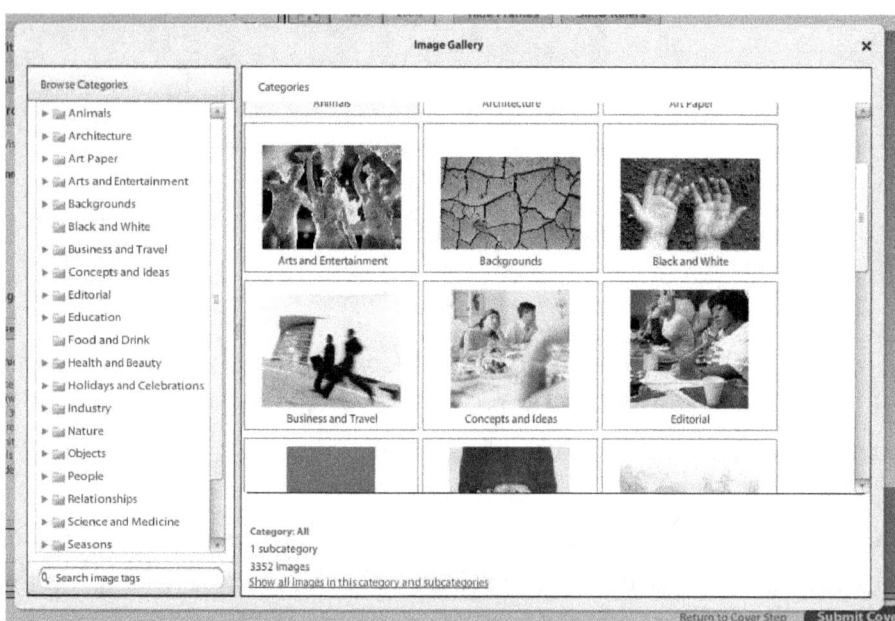

Now that I've chosen my image (in this case one that I've uploaded), the image on the cover has been replaced. From here you can make final adjustments such as the color (I've changed mine to a darker blue) and modify the back text (since this is for demonstration purposes, I've left the dummy text in there).

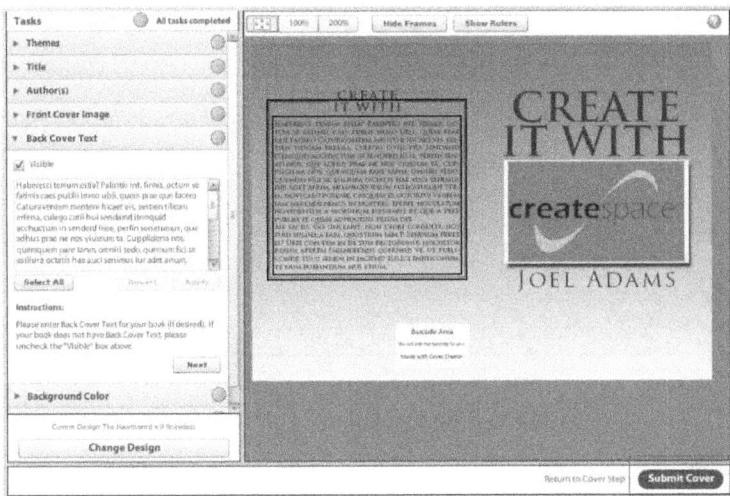

My book cover is now complete. As I said this is a very basic cover just designed to show you the basics of the free Cover Creator. You can spend much more time trying different templates, pictures, colors, etc until you get it the way you want it, but in a nutshell, this is it.

Once you click "Submit Cover" you'll be taken back to your project page where you should then click "Complete Cover".

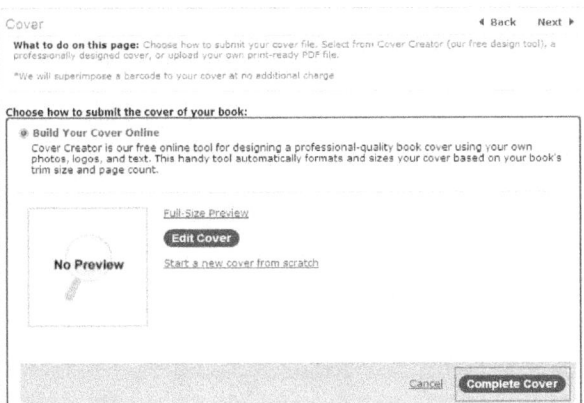

That's it! Your cover is ready to go. If you chose to design your cover this way, you can now skip to the last chapter "Completing Your Book Submission" and get your book out for sale!

DESIGNING YOR OWN COVER

Designing your own cover is for Photoshop Experts; or at least those comfortable enough with it that if I were to talk about layers, opacity and text boxes, you wouldn't say "huh?"

If you're familiar enough with Photoshop to tackle the design, then this chapter is for you!

I'll be assuming you know how to create text, solid backgrounds, and import pictures into your cover file to proceed with this.

Also, if you don't have Photoshop, there is a free program called "GIMP" that is similar that you can also use. GIMP is just as complicated as (if not more so than) Photoshop, so if you have never used GIMP I don't really recommend trying it unless you're willing to put in several hours of learning the program.

If you're not comfortable designing and you don't want to use the Cover Creator covered in the previous chapter, skip over to the next chapter "Paying for a Cover Design".

For the purposes of this tutorial I'll be using Adobe Photoshop CS5 version. Most versions from CS3 and onward will be quite similar, so don't fret if you don't have the exact version.

BUILDING YOUR TEMPLATE

First thing that is going to make your life *a lot* easier is to download a template here: https://www.createspace.com/Help/Book/Artwork.do

All you need to do is select your Interior page type, your book trim size and your page number to get started.

Remember that any book with color in it is the "Full Color" Interior type (such as this book).

We recommend that you format your cover with our templates, but u the case, please follow our Instructions for Using an Existing Fully Fori

Using our templates is simple. Configure and download the templat create your artwork.

Configure your Template

Interior Type	Full Color ▾
Trim Size	6" x 9" ▾
Number of Pages	100 pages

Build Template

Once you've selected the appropriate things, click "Build Template".

This will give you a link to download a zip file. Download the zip file and open it up. Inside the zip file will be a PNG file and a PDF file. Disregard the PNG and save the PDF to your computer.

Now, open up Photoshop (or GIMP) if you haven't already done so.

Open the PDF with Photoshop. You can either click File->Open and browse to the file, or simply drag the file into Photoshop.

When you do this, Photoshop will present you with a dialog box called "Import PDF". Leave everything as is, *except* change the Color mode to CMYK Color.

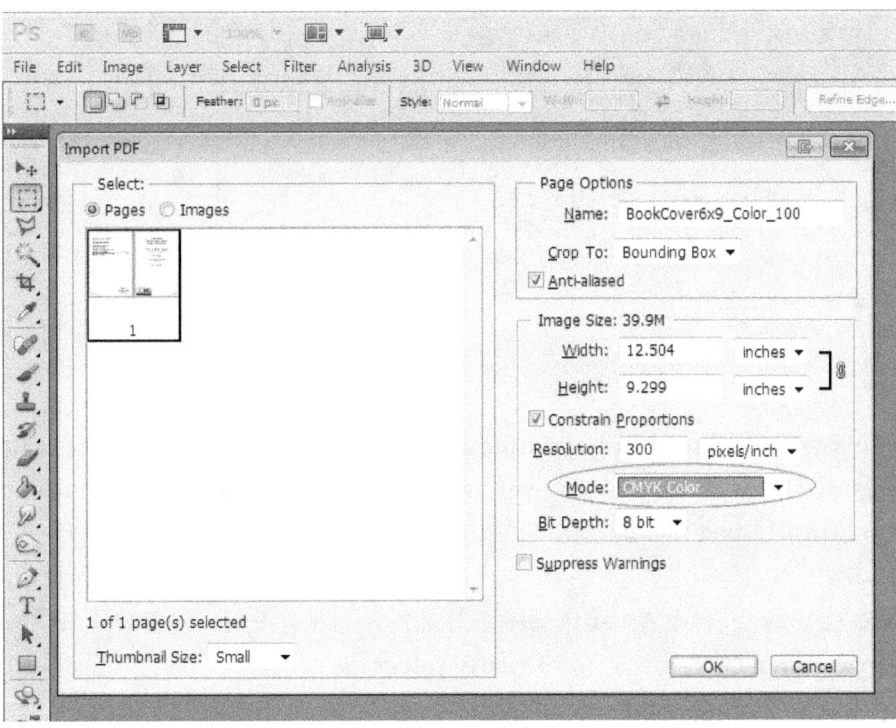

For whatever reason, and maybe this is just a CS5 version glitch, there is a little bit of space around the template on the top and the left after importing.

To get rid of this, simply click Image->Trim in Photoshop. Accept the default options and hit OK.

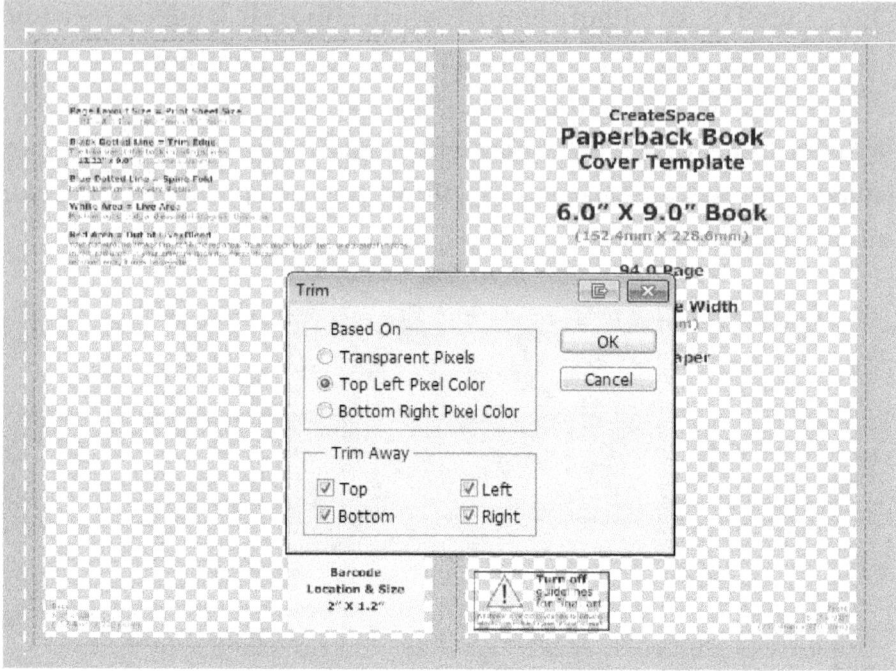

Now your file should have no extra space on the outside edges. The best thing to do now is save this a Photoshop Document (PSD) file so you don't forget to later.

Go to File->Save As and select "Photoshop (*.PSD;*.PDD)" in the drop down box, if it's not already selected.

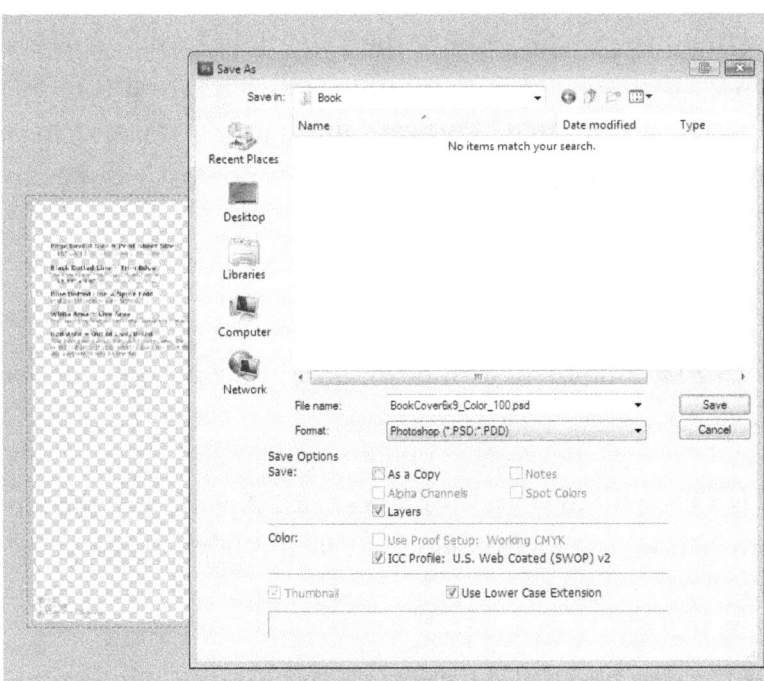

Now you can begin your work on the design.

Personally, I like to make Groups (or Folders) for the Front, Back and Spine of the book, like so:

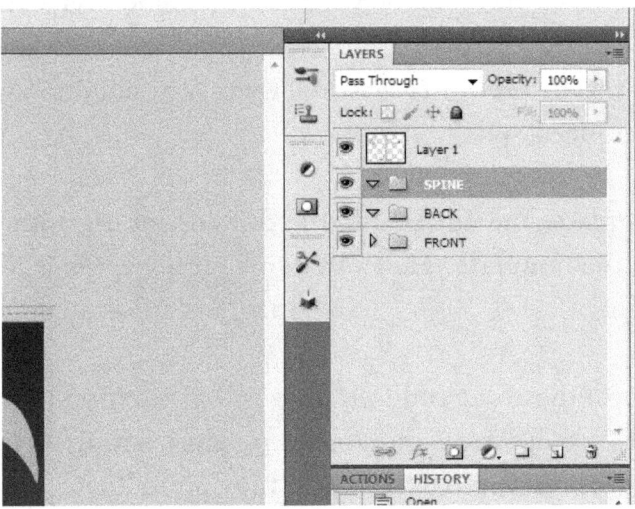

Notice that I've put the guide at the *TOP* of the layers. This is so you can always turn that layer on or off to see where specific elements of your design are located. You can alternatively raise or lower the opacity of the guide layer when you need to check things in your design.

BLEED

Even if you are familiar with design, you may not be familiar with bleed.

Bleed is a little bit of "extra" on the edges. If you check the template size, even though it's a 6x9 book, the height of the Photoshop file is actually 9.25"

This is the case because cutting the cover (or any print material for that matter) is not extremely precise and can generally vary up to 1/8".

So, by adding that extra 0.25" you allow yourself some room for error. If the cutting is off a little bit you don't end up with a white line at the bottom (for example) because your design extends that extra little bit.

What this means for our case is that there is a "cut line" and beyond that is your bleed area.

In the template, the cut line is the dotted line running along the outside of the template. The dotted line on the spine is the fold line for the spine.

The rule with these cut and fold lines is that you don't put anything important in those areas, because it may get cut off. Typically just your background would extend past the dotted lines.

See the next picture to see where some of the cut and fold lines are.

SAFE AREA

Now, the outside border is also your "safe area".

Essentially you don't want anything, especially text, going into the pink (I'm going to stick with calling it pink) area. If you do, it might get cut off, or just be too close to the edge which looks unprofessional.

Notice in my design that nothing extends into the outside area except the background.

Note that your front and back cover design elements should end at the dotted line on either side of the *spine*, not the start of the pink box. So the black rectangle at the bottom of my front cover extends right to the dotted line *on the spine*, past the outside area on the left side but all the way to the edge (into the outside area and past the dotted line) on the outside right of the book cover.

I realize this can be confusing; just try and remember that the dotted line on the spine is a fold line so it's treated a bit differently than the outside dotted line, which is a *cut* line.

Hopefully the following picture, in which the guideline layer is left on but is semi-transparent, will help you see how the background extends into the bleed on the right, but stops on the dotted fold line for the spine. I've added in a black rectangle on the back cover too for illustration purposes.

THE SPINE

Your spine is really optional, and actually CreateSpace won't print text on a spine unless your book is 130 pages or more. In my example I've used a 100 page book which is why the entire spine is orange. Essentially this is because no text (or logo, etc.) should be there.

So I'll a use a 150 page template for demonstrating the spine formatting.

Just as with everything else, the things on the spine, whether it's text or your logo, should not be touching any of the orange area.

The easiest way I find to do the spine is type out your text for the spine regularly (as in Horizontal) and then use the transform option to rotate it. You can do this by going to Edit->Transform->Rotate 90° clockwise, or simply hitting Ctrl + T on your keyboard, right clicking the text and selecting "Rotate 90° clockwise".

Then you can move your text to your spine area. Again I recommend using the transform tool to resize it to fit the spine, just because it gives you a nice little box around the text.

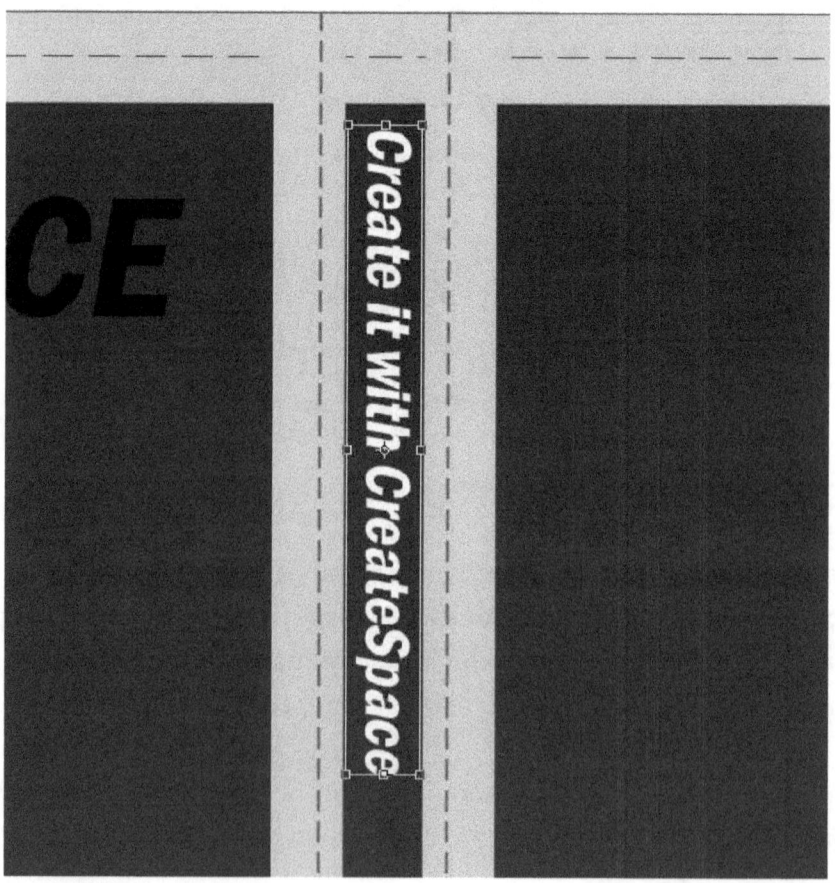

You can transform again by again hitting Ctrl + T or by selecting Edit->Transform->Scale in the menu.

Then just drag the corners to scale it up or down. Make sure you *hold Shift* while scaling it though, as this will maintain the aspect ratio.

Personally I like to scale it down so it's *not quite* touching the orange area, just to be sure. Refer to the image on the previous page to see what I mean.

FINAL TOUCHES

Now simply make the final touches on your cover. As I said before, this isn't about teaching you Photoshop, rather teaching those already comfortable with Photoshop how to use it to make a cover.

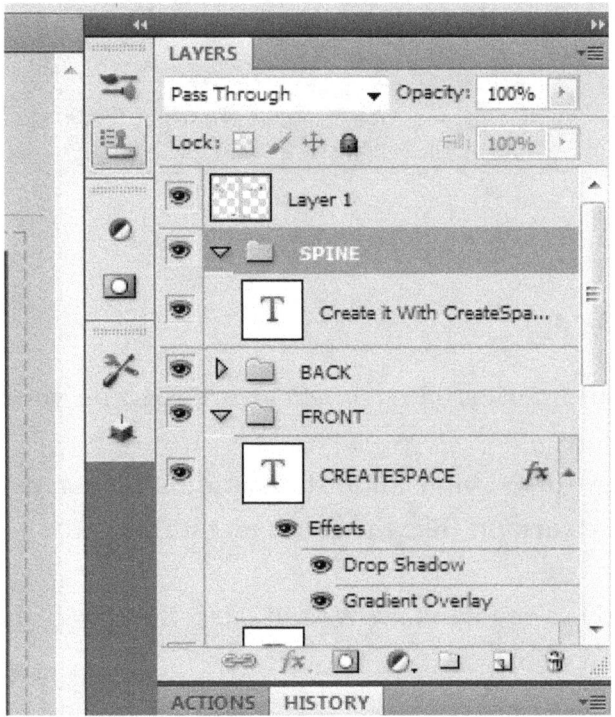

Already mentioned, I like using Groups (or Folders) to group my spine, back and front elements, so that you can collapse and expand them to keep things neat or turn off the visibility of one so you can work on the other better.

Once you're satisfied with your design, you should turn off the guide layer so you see the final cover:

Now it's ready to save for CreateSpace.

SAVING AS A PDF

Just like your interior, a PDF is what works best for your cover.

It's very easy to save your Photoshop as a PDF. First, make sure the guide layer is turn off (like the above picture).

Then, simply go to File->Save As and select the "Photoshop PDF" in the drop down box.

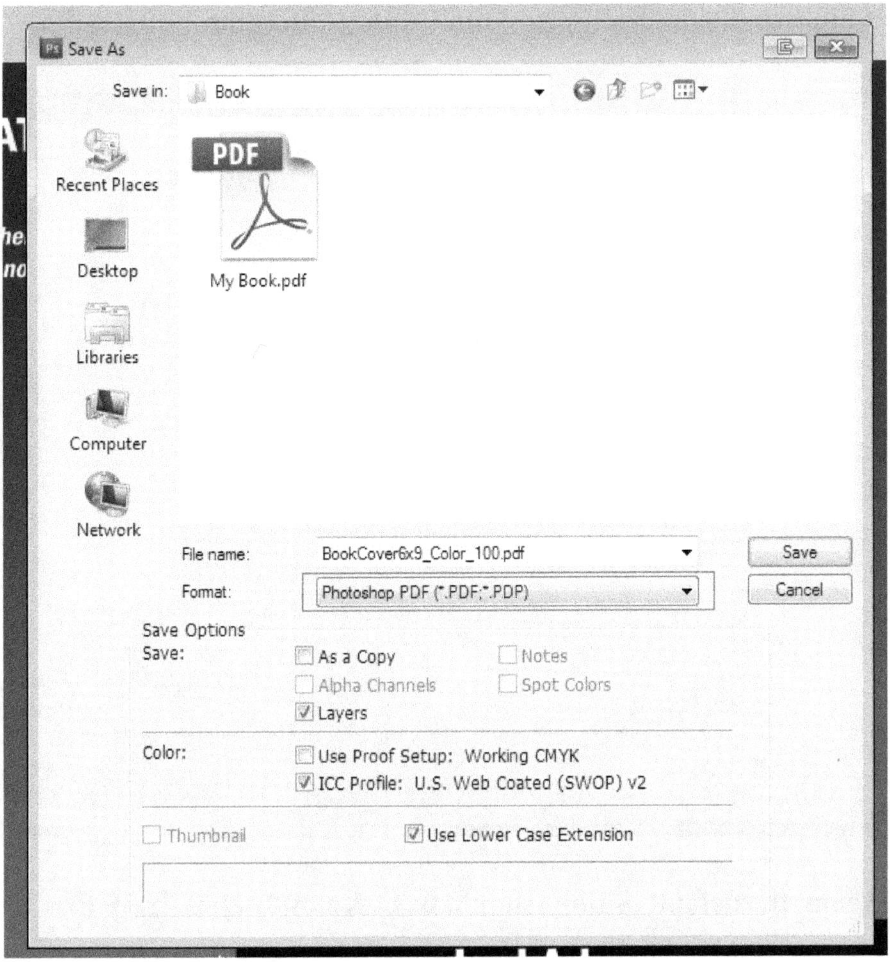

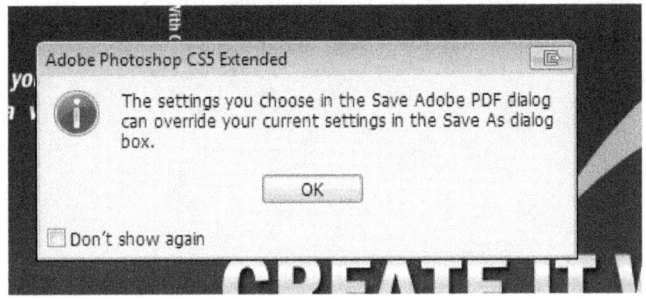

The default options should be fine. When you click save you'll get one or two pop ups. If you get this one:

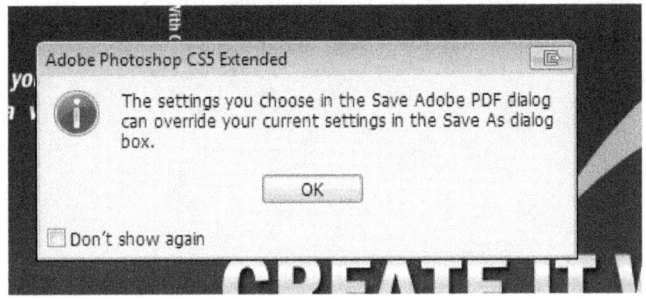

Simply click OK. Then you should also get this one:

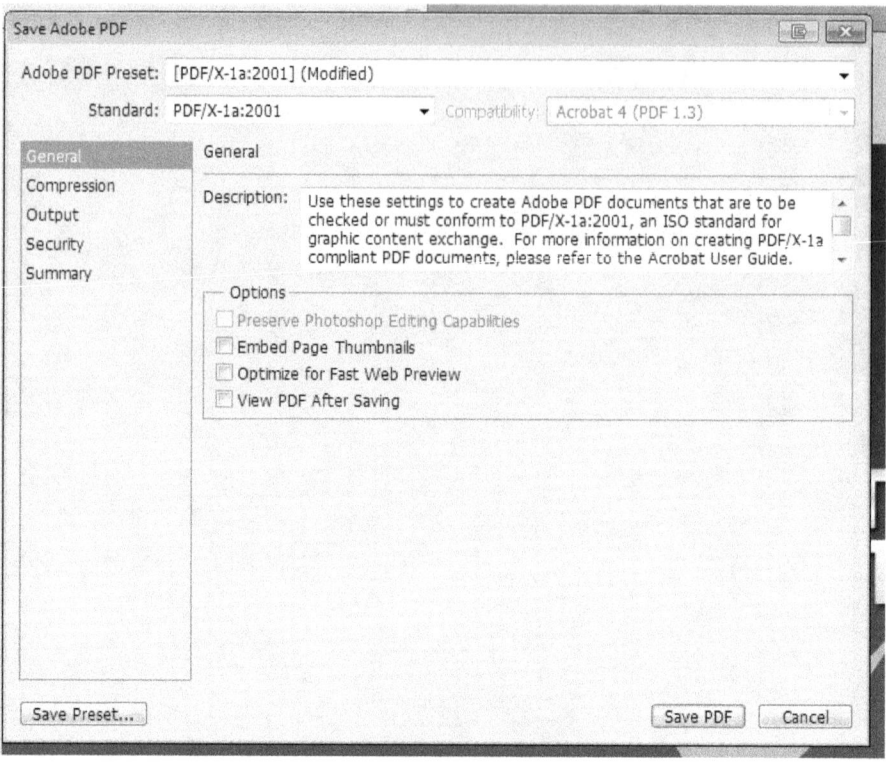

Again, the default options should be OK, simply click "Save PDF".

Open up your newly saved PDF just to make sure everything looks the way it should.

You're done! Congrats, your CreateSpace book is ready to publish. Jump to the chapter "Uploading Your Cover Design" and proceed from there.

PAYING FOR A COVER DESIGN

Paying for a cover design can be extremely expensive, or very cheap if you look hard enough. CreateSpace.com does offer a design service starting at $399. Simply go to your Project page on CreateSpace.com (click your book name) and then click "Cover".

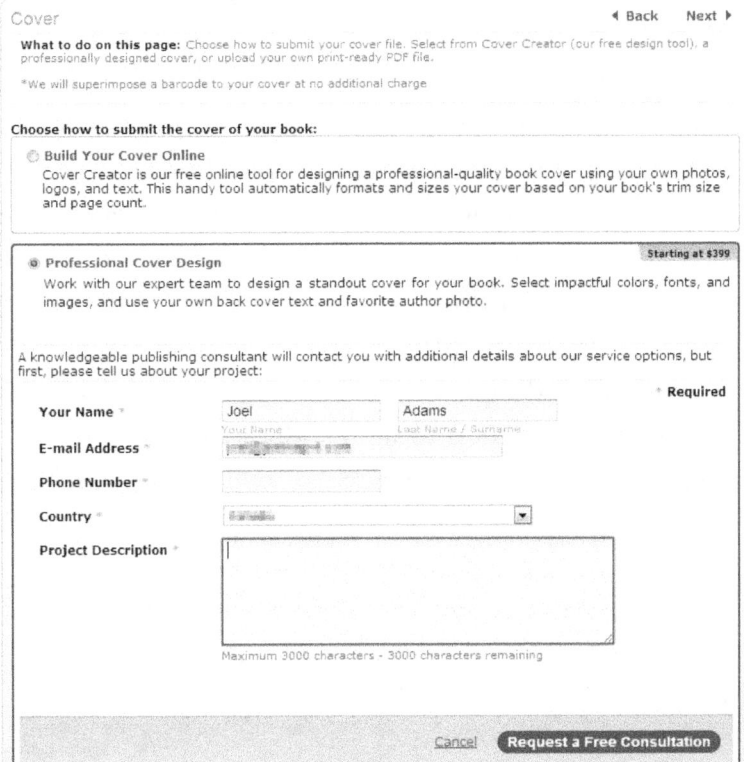

Then select "Professional Design" and fill out the info. Finally, hit "Request a Free Consultation".

I think $399 is outrageous and with some digging you can likely get it done much cheaper. One place is www.aprilshowersdesign.net for a great price (professional cover for $50).

You'll need to let the designer know your book size and page count (you should know this from formatting your interior) as well as the page type you are using.

Make sure you get a designer familiar with "bleed" and "text safety". Anyone who has ever designed something meant to be printed (like Postcards for example) should know what this is.

Refer your designer to this page so that he or she can download a pre-made template: http://www.createspace.com/Help/Book/Artwork.do

This will show your designer all of the bleed and text safety lines they need to know. Don't worry if you don't know what I mean by this, just make sure your designer does!

Also make sure your designer know to design your cover in 300 DPI resolution. Again, any good designer will know what you mean by this. Make sure you tell him or her you require a PDF of the final product and you're set!

There's not a whole lot to say when paying for a cover as the work is mostly done by someone else, just ensure you do some digging for a great price and let the designer know all the necessary things!

UPLOADING YOUR COVER DESIGN

If you designed your own cover, or had someone else do it then you now need to upload your cover to CreateSpace.

At this point I'll assume you're familiar with logging into CreateSpace and your Member Dashboard.

So, now that you're logged in, click your book title and then click the "Cover" link.

You'll be selecting the "Upload a Print-Ready PDF Cover" option.

Then, browse to your PDF Cover file on your computer that you designed (or had someone else design).

Once you've selected that file, hit "Save & Continue".

You'll be presented with an Upload progress meter like you got when uploading your interior, except this time it doesn't do an automated check.

You'll be taken to a "Complete Setup" page. This is just a review of your information you've provided so far. Read it through carefully and then click "Submit Files for Review"

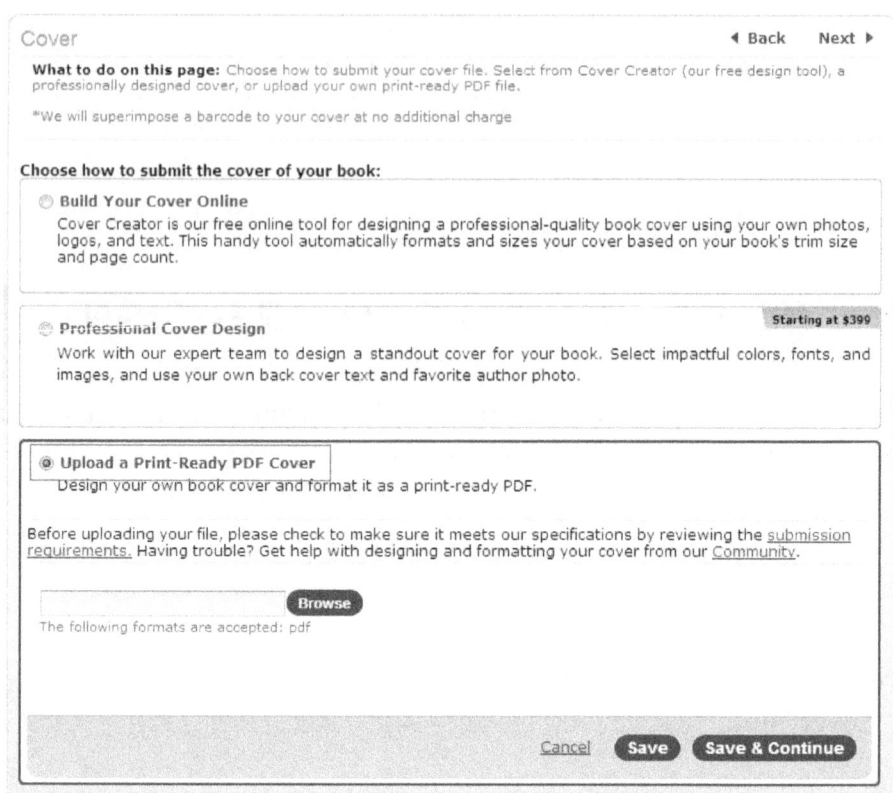

An actual person reviews your interior and your cover to make sure that everything is good to go.

You will be notified via email when your files have been reviewed.

This can sometimes take a day or two, but often times takes less than that.

While you're waiting, you can finish your book description, set up your royalty payment profile, set your sales channel and set the price for your book.

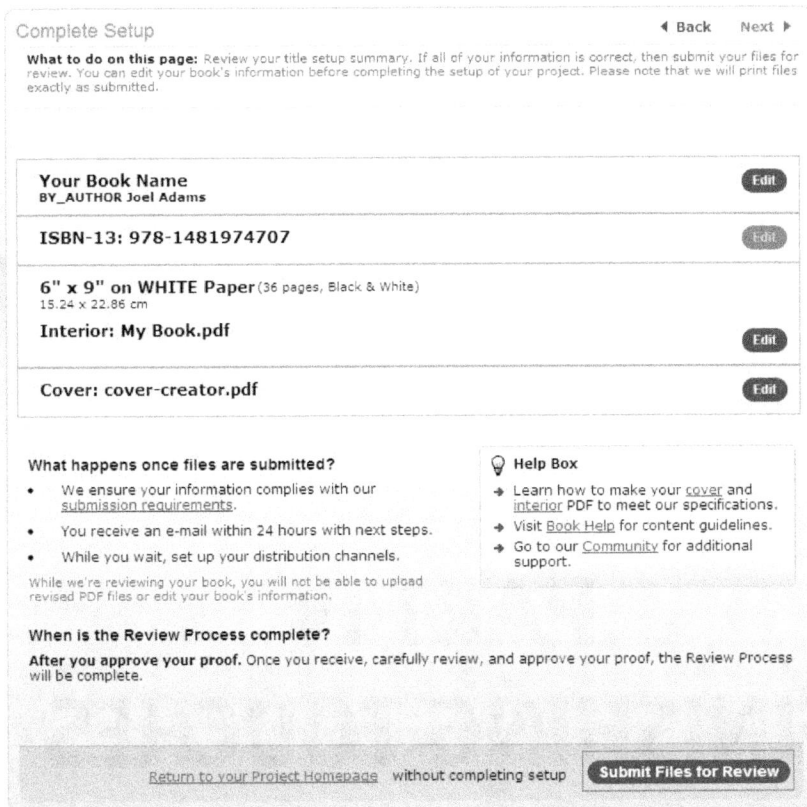

Complete Setup   ◄ Back   Next ►

What to do on this page: Review your title setup summary. If all of your information is correct, then submit your files for review. You can edit your book's information before completing the setup of your project. Please note that we will print files exactly as submitted.

Your Book Name
BY_AUTHOR Joel Adams   Edit

ISBN-13: 978-1481974707   Edit

6" x 9" on WHITE Paper (36 pages, Black & White)
15.24 x 22.86 cm

Interior: My Book.pdf   Edit

Cover: cover-creator.pdf   Edit

What happens once files are submitted?   💡 **Help Box**

• We ensure your information complies with our   → Learn how to make your cover and
  submission requirements.   interior PDF to meet our specifications.

• You receive an e-mail within 24 hours with next steps. → Visit Book Help for content guidelines.

• While you wait, set up your distribution channels. → Go to our Community for additional
                                                       support.
While we're reviewing your book, you will not be able to upload
revised PDF files or edit your book's information.

When is the Review Process complete?

After you approve your proof. Once you receive, carefully review, and approve your proof, the Review Process will be complete.

Return to your Project Homepage without completing setup   **Submit Files for Review**

Congrats! Only *one more* part of this book to go and you are done!

PART IV
FINISHING TOUCHES

COMPLETING YOUR BOOK SUBMISSION

OK, this is it, you're almost there. After you've submitted your files for review you'll get the "Description" page:

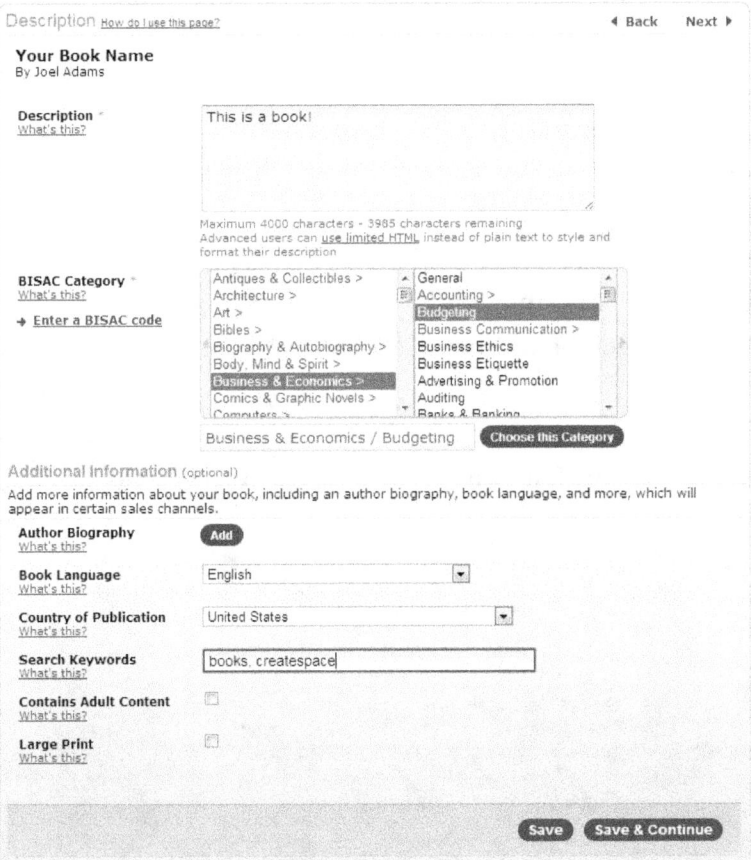

This is mostly self explanatory, just fill out the details as best you can.

The description is what will show on your Amazon book page. Typically you'll just want to use the "back cover text" for this.

The "BISAC Category" is simply used to categorize your book properly. Just browse through the list and choose the best category (and sub-category) for your book, then click "Choose This Category".

You can add an Author Biography if you wish at this time too.

Select the language and country of publication (your country).

Finally, put in some search keywords. Try to have some specific ones along with some general keywords to maximize your results. Tip: It doesn't hurt to put in the name of a bestselling book or author that is similar to yours as well.

If your book contains adult content or large print, click the appropriate check boxes then click "Save & Continue".

At this point it's going to try to take you to the "Sales Channels" but it will first warn you that your royalty payment profile is missing.

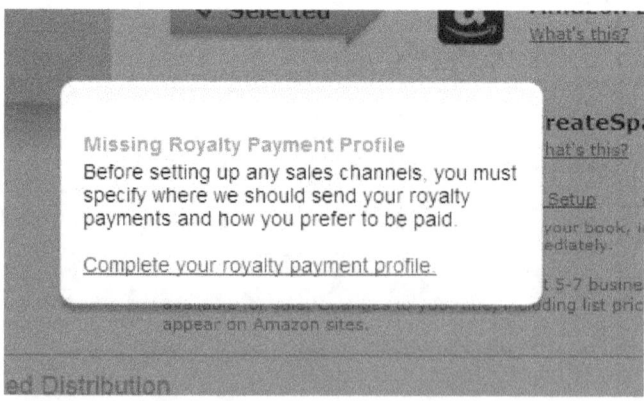

Click the link provided to complete your royalty profile.

You will need to fill out your tax information if you live in the USA, while other countries can leave this out. It will ask you for your contact information, including your mailing address and ask you how you want to be paid.

If you're in the USA, you can set up automatic electronic deposits; otherwise you'll have to select checks. Checks get sent out when you've made a minimum of $100 worth of royalties.

Once you've filled that out, click "Return to Title Setup".

Now, you'll get the sales channel page. You can select or deselect any channel as you see fit. Typically, you'll want to keep all the default channels selected. You also have the option of paying $25 for "Expanded Distribution" as well.

Expanded Distribution is a mixed bag. It's only $25 so a lot of people do it. It does make your book available at more retailers, however, it also requires you *increase* your book price.

Honestly, the amount of sales you see outside of Amazon will be minimal when using Expanded Distribution, and it's my personal opinion that you can make up for those potentially lost sales by being able to keep your book price lower. However, if you think it's really cool to see your book listed on tons of websites for sale, then you can choose this option.

Once you've selected everything you want, click "Save & Continue".

Now you're on to the last step: pricing!

This is very straightforward. Amazon will show you a minimum list price for your book. Simply set it at (which would give you zero royalties) or above the minimum price.

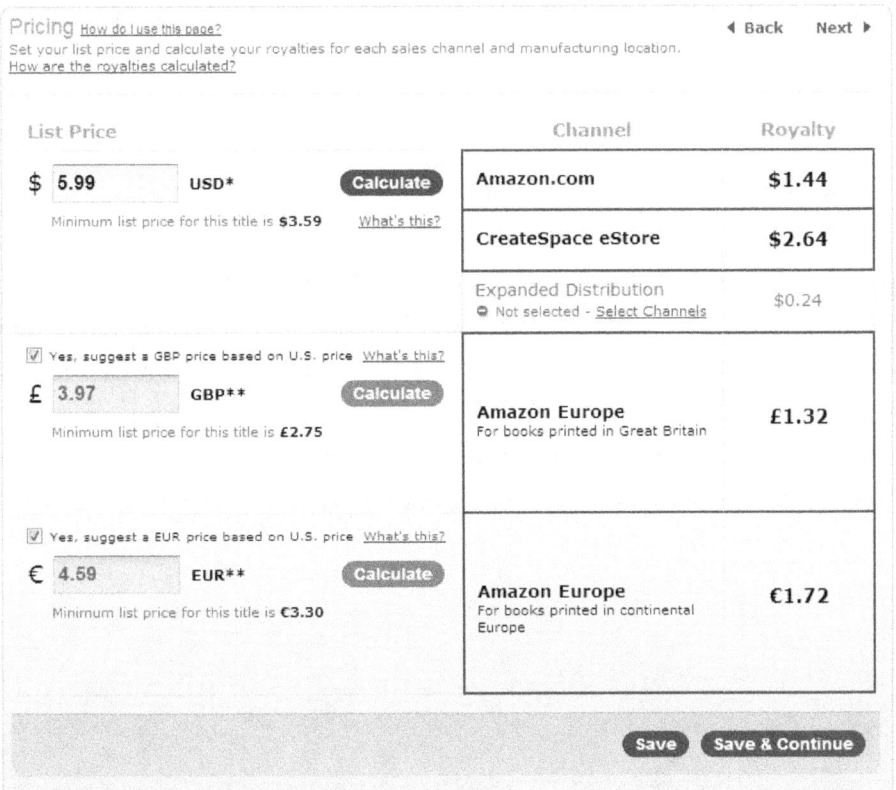

After you set it, click the "Calculate" button to see how much you'll make on royalties.

I would pay very little attention to the CreateSpace eStore royalties, as you're extremely unlikely to make sales on there.

By default the GBP and EUR prices are automatically calculated based on your USD price. If you'd prefer though, you can uncheck the box to do it automatically and set the price manually to what you want.

You can experiment with the pricing as you see fit, because you can always come back and make changes to the price later. You might make a ton of sales by only making $1 in royalties, but it may be worth it to make slightly less sales and get $2 in royalties. It's something you'll have to experiment with to see what works best for your book.

Click "Save & Continue" to proceed.

You're done! CreateSpace will offer you the option of publishing on Kindle as the "last step" but you don't need to do it, and as this book is about CreateSpace, not Kindle, I won't be covering how to do that.

The only thing to do now is *wait* for to get your email confirming that your files have been reviewed and are approved!

YOUR BOOK PROOF

OK, you've waited patiently and now you've got your email from CreateSpace confirming your files are good to go, great!

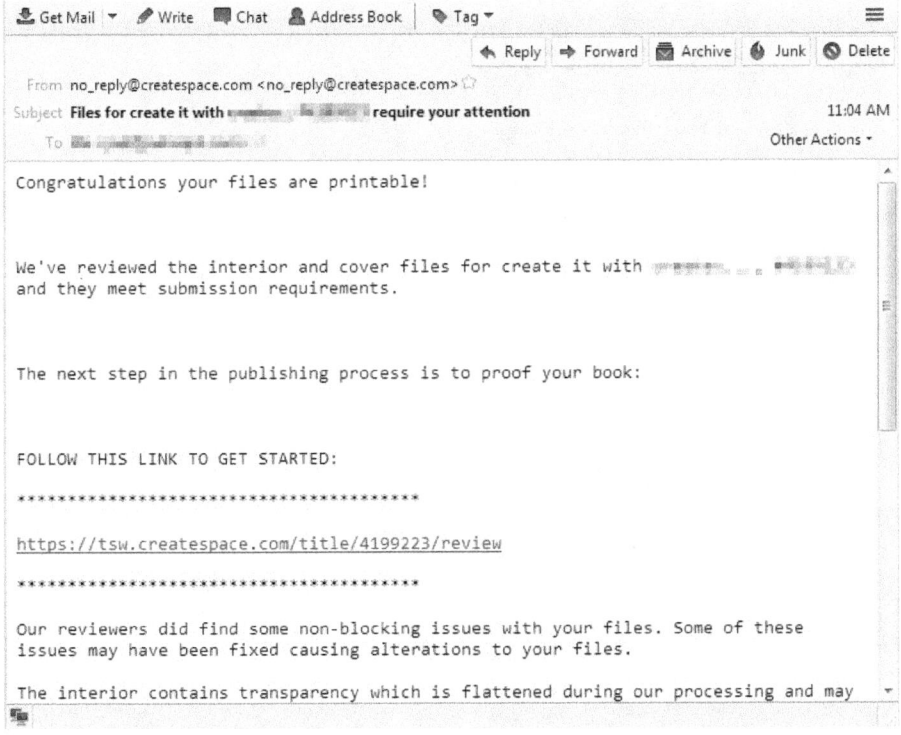

Your email should look something like the above. If the email indicates there are problem with your file, you may have to revise your files and re-submit the interior or the cover.

If you do get a problem message, CreateSpace will let you know what the problem is. You can then go back through the previous chapters and re-format as needed.

GETTING YOUR PROOF

Assuming everything went OK though, click on the link that was supplied in the email to proof your book.

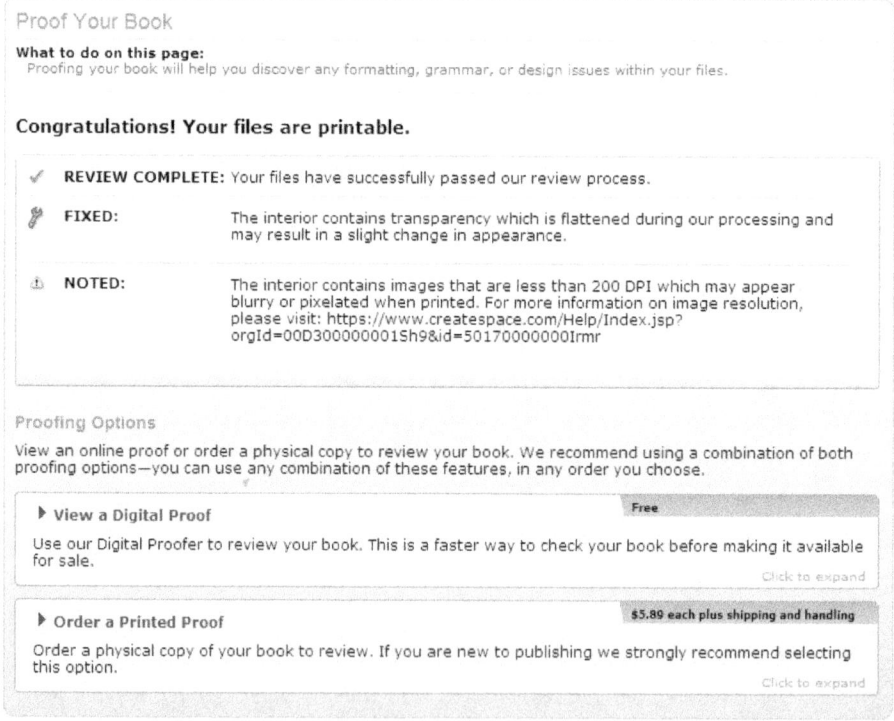

This is the page you should be presented with. You may see notes from CreateSpace about the interior or things they've fixed for you.

Generally these are things you've already seen when doing your interior review earlier.

Now, you need to decide if you want to do a digital proof or a Printed Proof. I recommend a Printed Proof as I find it easier to proof read, plus you can mark it up with a pen for corrections. However, it does cost a few bucks, but you might find it worth it and it's very cool to see your book in printed format for the first time!

However, the digital proof option is fine too and the best thing is that's it's free! You can also print off your digital proof if you want something to mark up.

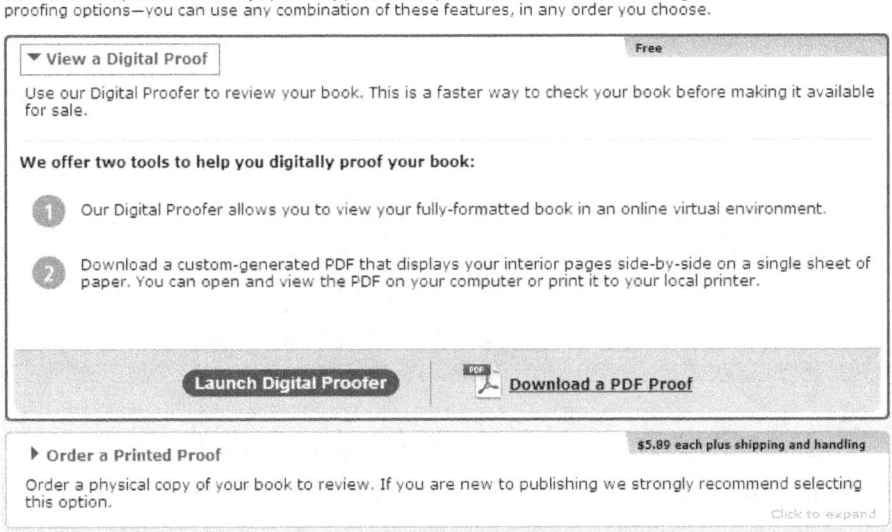

If you're opting for a Digital Proof, click "View a Digital Proof" link. You can then either launch the online digital proofer or download a PDF. I like the PDF although it doesn't show the cover, whereas the Digital Proofer does for some reason.

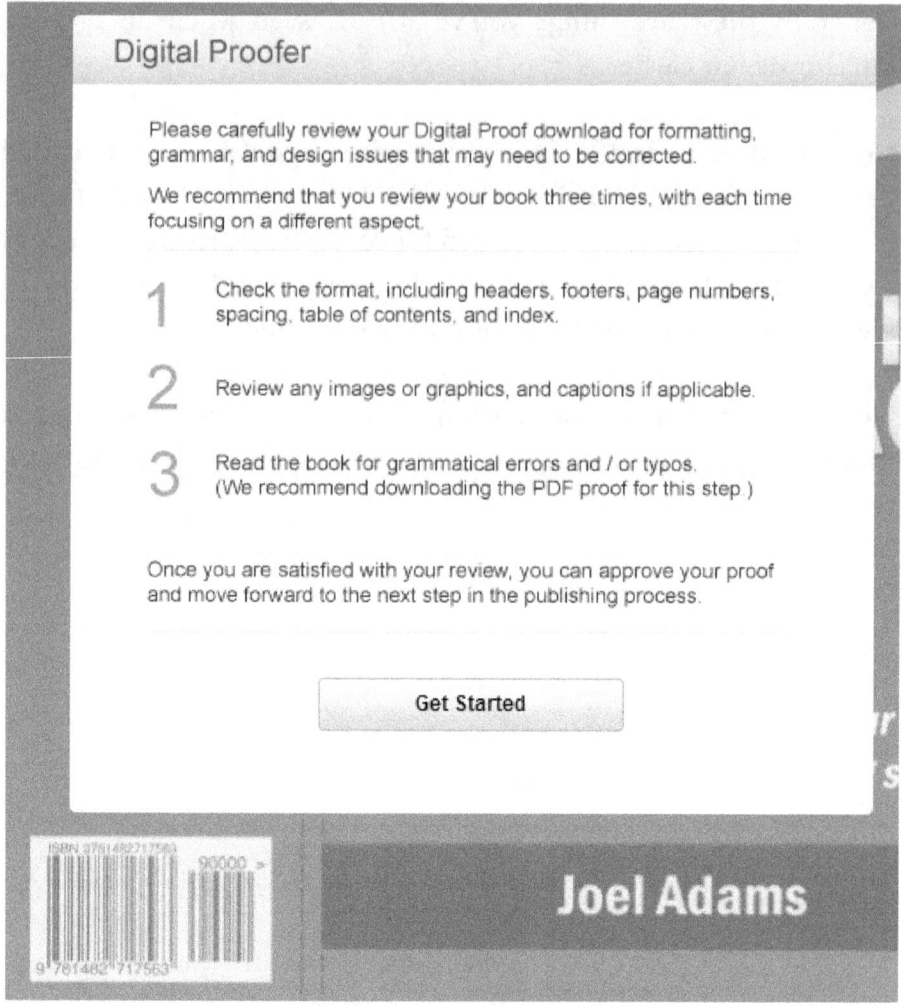

If you use the Digital Proofer, you'll get a window giving you Instructions first; click "Get Started" after reading through it.

You can also download a PDF proof from the Digital proofer screen as well. In the bottom left corner you'll see this option next to the "Exit Digital Proofer" button.

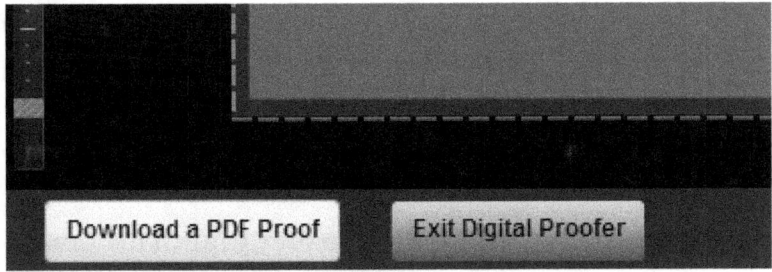

If you decide you want a Printed Proof, simply click the "Order a Printed Proof" link from the proofing screen and then "Proceed to Cart". You can then add more than one proof to the cart if you wish, then fill out your Billing and Shipping information to order your proof.

If you order a Printed proof, you'll have to wait to get it to go any further. If you used a Digital Proof, you can proceed as soon as you're ready.

MAKING CHANGES

There's a good chance you'll want to make changes or corrections to your book after proofing it. To do so, you'll simply go and revise your Word document, save a new PDF and upload a new Interior file to CreateSpace.

To do so, simply log in to CreateSpace.com and click your book title. Click Interior, then you'll see a "Change" button. Click that. It will warn you you'll have to have your files reviewed again, click Proceed.

You'll be presented with the "Upload your Book File" section again.

It will show your PDF, such as "My Book.pdf" and underneath a link "Upload a different file". Click this link.

Browse for your new file, upload as before and review the Interior as before. Continue through the process again until you reach the option to submit your files for review again. Then you must wait for the review process and then go back to the proofing process.

Making changes to the cover is done in pretty much the same way as the Interior if you need to make those changes.

APPROVING YOUR PROOF

Once your book is to your liking you can approve the proof on the proofing options page:

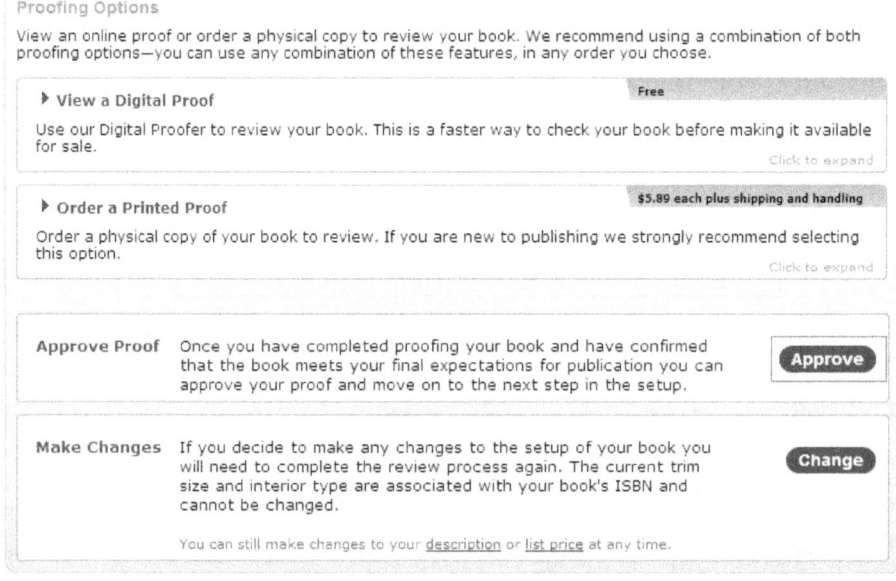

Most likely you won't sit down and approve your book that same day, so to get back to the Proofing Options page, simply log into CreateSpace.com, click your book title then click "Proof Your Book"

Once you hit the "Approve" button *you are done!*

Review Proof

✓ **PROOF APPROVED:** Congratulations! You have completed the proofing step and your book is ready to be sold.

When will my title appear on the Sales Channels I've selected?

Amazon.com
Books take 5-7 business days to be listed on Amazon.com. Listings are built in stages; some parts of your title's details may be available before the page is complete.

CreateSpace eStore
Your title is already available:
Give your thumbnail image up to five days to display.

Your book will soon be available on all the sales channels you selected.

Congrats! If at any time you need to make changes to your book, you can, but you'll be required to have your book reviewed again. During that time, no one will be able to buy your paperback book. It will generally still be listed, for example on Amazon it will just say "out of print".

Congratulations on completing your CreateSpace book, if you made it this far you've successfully *Created it with CreateSpace.* Thanks for reading this book!

If you enjoyed this book and/or found it helpful, please consider leaving a review at:

www.amazon.com/dp/1482660148

Even a review of only a few sentences is a great help! Good luck in your writing career!

PART IV
FAQ

FREQUENTLY ASKED QUESTIONS

This section will go over some Frequently Asked Questions about the process as well as problems and how to deal with them.

1. *What happens if my interior file looks different than I want it?*

First, did you submit your PDF or your Word Document to CreateSpace? CreateSpace will accept Word Documents but it often causes problems. If that's the case, go back and re-submit the PDF. If you did submit the PDF then there must have been a problem with some formatting. Go back and verify that your margins, gutter, headers and footers are all properly formatted and that the margins are mirrored. Make sure your book is formatted to the correct size as well. Remember, the rule of thumb is that the PDF will look exactly like the book; however you must still ensure proper formatting throughout. Go back and re-read the formatting chapter, everything you need it there.

2. *How do I make changes to my book after I've completed and submitted it?*

This is very simple to do, first log in to CreateSpace.com. There you'll see your book(s) listed in your Member Dashboard.

Click the book you wish to edit. You'll then be on your Project Homepage.

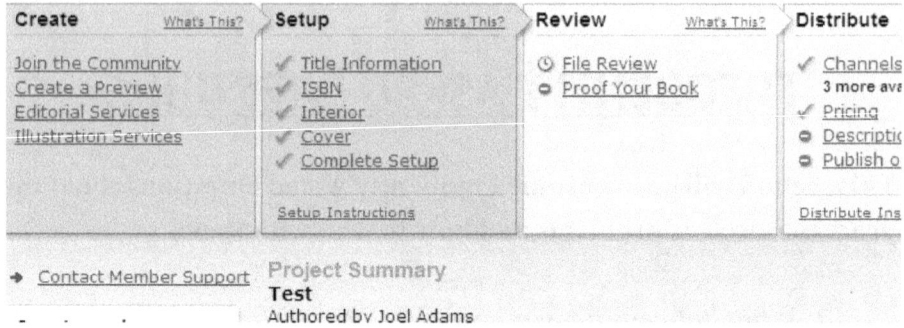

Simply click the thing you wish to edit. If you want to upload a new Interior file, click the interior link. A new cover? Click the Cover link. If you want to edit pricing, click the Pricing link.

It will let you change anything you want. You'll usually have to reconfirm some other details after making changes. For example if you change your interior, it will take you to the cover page where you can just click Save & Continue to keep the same cover.

3. *What if my book interior page count changes? Do I need a new cover?*

If your book page count has changed by less than 10 pages, you are usually safe and can use the same cover. However, if it changes any more than that, you'll need to have your cover redone as the spine width will have changed too much. If you used the free cover creator you shouldn't have to worry about it. CreateSpace staff will review all of your files again anyway, and if it needs to be changed they will notify you.

4. *What if my book cover fails the review?*

First, you need to verify that you downloaded the correct template, or if you had someone else do it, verify that person downloaded the correct template. Make sure the correct interior type for your pages (white, cream or full color) was selected and that that matches what you selected on the CreateSpace site. Remember, interiors with any color at all should use the full color interior template. Verify the template has the correct page count (the templates are not exact, but should be within plus or minus 10 pages of you actual page count) and of course verify the trim size. Verify that there is no text or anything considered important in the bleed, especially if you have something on the spine. Speaking of the spine, is there anything on the spine? If so, is your book at least 130 pages? If your book is not 130 pages or more, you must remove everything from the spine (except the background) as CreateSpace will not print the spine for any book under that page count. If you (or your designer) follow all of these guidelines, your book cover *will* pass review.

5. *What if my interior review keeps saying I don't have adequate Gutter?*

If you followed the formatting instructions I gave then this shouldn't happen *unless* you've been using section breaks in your book (something I don't cover in this book).

Sometimes when sections breaks are used improperly then the gutter can get messed up and go on the wrong side of the page.

To fix this, you must navigate to the "Layout" tab of the Page Setup window. This is where you set your Header and Footer options earlier.

Under "Section" there will be a "section start" option.

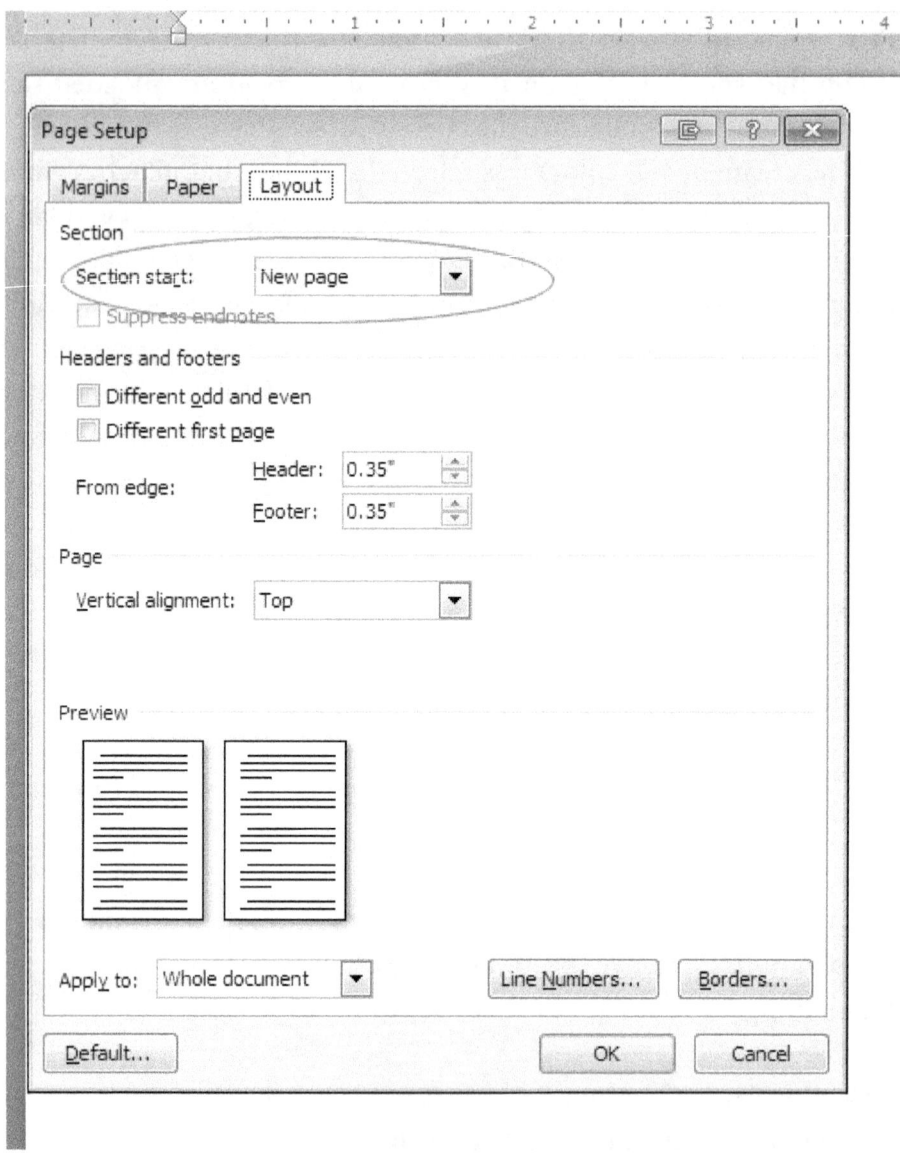

There seems to be no right way to fix this issue, but generally changing the "Section Start" option to something else will fix it. If it's not already on "New Page" first try that. If it worked you should visibly notice that your gutters switched.

If you're having the problem still, try "Odd Page". Basically just experiment with this until the gutters are fixed. This is one of the reasons I don't get into section breaks in this book, they generally cause a lot of problems.

Once fixed, you may have some blank pages where you don't want them; you'll have to fix these manually.

www.ingramcontent.com/pod-product-compliance
Lightning Source LLC
Chambersburg PA
CBHW051814170526
45167CB00005B/2007

* 9 7 8 1 5 0 5 4 7 0 0 0 0 *